ENCOUNTERING
GOD

Cultivating Habits of Faith
Through the Spiritual Disciplines

KELLY MINTER

Lifeway Press®
Nashville, Tennessee

EDITORIAL TEAM, LIFEWAY WOMEN BIBLE STUDIES

Becky Loyd
Director,
Lifeway Women

Tina Boesch
Manager, Lifeway
Women Bible Studies

Sarah Doss
Lifeway Women Bible
Studies Team Leader

Mike Wakefield
Content Editor

Erin Franklin
Production Editor

Lauren Ervin
Art Director

Published by Lifeway Press® • © 2021 Kelly Minter
Reprinted February 2022

ISBN: 978-1-0877-3041-7

Item: 005829509

Dewey decimal classification: 234.2

Subject heading: DISCIPLESHIP / SPIRITUAL LIFE / FAITH

Unless otherwise noted, all Scripture quotations are taken from the Christian Standard Bible®, Copyright © 2017 by Holman Bible Publishers. Used by permission. Christian Standard Bible® and CSB® are federally registered trademarks of Holman Bible Publishers. Scripture quotations marked (ESV) are from the ESV® Bible (The Holy Bible, English Standard Version®), copyright © 2001 by Crossway, a publishing ministry of Good News Publishers. Some Scripture quotations are from THE MESSAGE. Copyright © by Eugene H. Peterson 1993, 1994, 1995, 1996, 2000, 2001, 2002. Used by permission of NavPress. All rights reserved. Represented by Tyndale House Publishers, Inc. Scripture quotations marked (NIV) are taken from the Holy Bible, New International Version®, NIV®.Copyright © 1973, 1978, 1984, 2011 by Biblica, Inc.™ Used by permission of Zondervan. All rights reserved worldwide. www.zondervan.com. The "NIV" and "New International Version" are trademarks registered in the United States Patent and Trademark Office by Biblica, Inc.™ Scripture marked NKJV taken from the New King James Version®. Copyright © 1982 by Thomas Nelson. Used by permission. All rights reserved.

To order additional copies of this resource, write Lifeway Resources Customer Service; One Lifeway Plaza; Nashville, TN 37234; FAX order to 615.251.5933; call toll-free 800.458.2772; email orderentry@lifeway.com; or order online at lifeway.com.

Printed in the United States of America

Lifeway Resources,
One Lifeway Plaza,
Nashville, TN 37234

TABLE OF CONTENTS

ENCOUNTERING GOD

ABOUT THE AUTHOR

Kelly is passionate about God's Word and believes it permeates all of life. The personal healing and steadfast hope she's found in the pages of Scripture fuels her passion to connect God's Word to our everyday lives. When she's not writing or teaching, you can find her tending her garden, taking a walk with friends, cooking for her nieces and nephews, riding a boat down the Amazon River, or walking through a Moldovan village with Justice & Mercy International (JMI).

Kelly's love for teaching Scripture led her to create her Cultivate Event, an event centered around Scripture, worship, prayer, and mission. She is also the host of the *Cultivate* podcast, a weekly podcast where she teaches the Bible in a conversational and approachable setting.

Kelly's past Bible studies include *Finding God Faithful: A Study on the Life of Joseph*; *No Other Gods: The Unrivaled Pursuit of Christ*; *All Things New: A Study on 2 Corinthians*; *What Love Is: The Letters of 1, 2 & 3 John*; *Nehemiah: A Heart That Can Break*; and *Ruth: Loss, Love & Legacy*. Kelly is also a singer-songwriter whose latest project is "Hymns & Hallelujahs."

Don't miss accompanying Kelly down the Amazon River on an unforgettable journey in her memoir, *Wherever The River Runs: How a Forgotten People Renewed My Hope in the Gospel*. Kelly partners with Justice & Mercy International, an organization that cares for the vulnerable and forgotten with the love of Jesus in the Amazon and Moldova. To find out more about JMI, visit justiceandmercy.org/cultivate. And to learn more about Kelly's Bible studies, books, music, and speaking schedule, visit kellyminter.com.

A WORD FROM KELLY

Here we are. At the beginning of a study on spiritual disciplines. Perhaps just the word *discipline* makes you want to sprint for the hills. Don't we all have enough to do already? Can't we just breathe? I understand this. We're absurdly busy, and life is a world-class jockey making us gallop to the pace of its whip. We want a nap, not more disciplines. But what if we discovered that practicing the spiritual disciplines can create more margin in our lives? What if we find that they're designed to instill peace, communion, and rest for our souls? What if we're not out of time—our priorities are just out of whack?

Somewhat surprisingly, I've found the spiritual disciplines to be liberating instead of cumbersome. We naturally think that piling on additional activities will only burden us further, yet practicing the spiritual disciplines daily reminds us that it's God we submit to, not life's relentless demands. This will require some effort on our part, but anything of value typically does. While absolutely nothing can be accomplished outside of God's grace and His Spirit, I sense we've adopted the misleading notion that we're supposed to work hard for all the "normal" things in our natural life, but our spirituality is supposed to just somehow happen. You know, by the power of the Spirit. We want God to transform us into His image. We want to sin less and serve more. We want to live generously and let go of our anger and cease worrying and have more peace, but we want God to snap His fingers and will it into existence.

We have little idea how to participate with Him or where to begin. We hope to achieve spiritual maturity the way Elisha scooped up Elijah's mantle that had literally fallen out of the sky (2 Kings 2:1-13). But when we go to Scripture, when we go to church history, we see that God very much invites our effort, our activity, our doing certain things in order to participate in our transformation. I fear that in our desire to rightly emphasize a godly posture of being, we have left out the biblical necessity of doing. This is where the spiritual disciplines come in.

Simply put, a discipline is "any activity I can do by direct effort that will eventually enable me to do that which, currently, I *cannot* do by direct effort."[1] Like a piano player who routinely practices her scales or a marathon runner who daily trains, eventually a run of notes turns into a recital of Beethoven, and 5 miles turns into 26.2. This is also true as it relates to being followers of Christ. The spiritual disciplines of solitude, prayer, Bible study, simplicity, worship, celebration, and more train us to do what we previously could not do as it relates to being conformed into the image of Jesus. The spiritual disciplines invite us, by God's grace, to change. They give us hope in our place of stuckness.

As we begin this adventure together, the key is to not get overwhelmed. Not all the spiritual disciplines can, or should be, practiced all at once. If we rested all the time, we'd never serve anyone. If we only studied Scripture, we wouldn't have time for prayer. And if we focused only on simplicity, when would we ever celebrate with a five-course meal we made from scratch? So there are times and places for each of the disciplines. Some will be daily habits such as Bible study, Scripture meditation, prayer, and worship. Others will be practiced at special times or in certain seasons, like when we fast, serve on a mission trip, or enter into solitude. Most of the spiritual disciplines are so closely related it's hard to know where one stops and the other begins. As we move in and out of the disciplines, it's less like turning off one road and onto another and more like a road changing names in the middle of the one you're already on. They're all part of the same path, and they all lead to the same Person, Jesus.

My hope is that through this study we'll learn what the Bible has to say about the spiritual disciplines. This understanding will give us the why behind these life-giving practices, which will inspire us toward implementing them into our daily lives. Above all, we'll discover that all those things about ourselves we think are impossible to change really can change. We're not stuck. Being transformed into the image of Christ is a practical reality— if we're willing to participate with Him through the blessing of discipline.

Kelly Minter

SESSION ONE

Introduction

WATCH SESSION ONE VIDEO

PSALM 90:1
PSALM 90:10
PSALM 90:12 WISDOM (NUMBER OUR DAYS)

DISCUSSION QUESTIONS

What drew you to this study on spiritual disciplines?

When you think about spiritual disciplines, what comes to mind?

How are the spiritual disciplines more about relationship than results? What happens if we make them just about results?

How do you think spiritual disciplines help us orient our lives around what really matters?

Take a quick look at the table of contents (p. 3). Which of the disciplines listed there are you most interested in? Why?

What do you hope to gain from this study?

SESSION TWO

Study

JOURNALING THE SESSION

Use this page throughout your session of study. We've given you some prompts, but feel free to write other thoughts and questions to help you learn and process the spiritual discipline of Bible study.

PREPARING FOR THE SESSION

Before you start your work this session, journal some of your thoughts about the discipline of Bible study. How have you practiced this discipline in the past? What has hindered your study of Scripture? What do you hope to get out of this session?

DURING THE SESSION

What are some key things you're learning this session about the discipline of Bible study?

REVIEWING THE SESSION

What are your biggest takeaways from this session, and how will you put them into practice?

Session Two Introduction

When it comes to studying the Bible, one of the first things we can get awfully excited about is that the God of the Bible is a speaking God. Since God is a speaking God and has spoken to us through His Word, studying the Bible is a thrilling endeavor. I did not say an easy one or even always a happy one—when I was in high school I flung my King James Version of the Bible across my bedroom because I was so mad at God for what He was saying to me. (Incidentally, the Bible also addresses anger, which ratcheted me up even more.) When we recognize that God still reveals Himself to us in our current day and speaks to us personally, studying the Bible becomes less of a dry discipline and more a living, breathing relationship where we commune with the living God. I can say without hesitation that meeting God through the pages of Scripture has been a dynamic journey that has touched every corner of my life. It has left no part of me alone.

So it is my highest honor to invite you to begin our study on the spiritual disciplines with perhaps the most foundational discipline of all, the study of Scripture. It's not that studying the Bible is more essential to our spiritual growth than say, prayer or worship, as much as it's the window through which God's light shines on all the other disciplines. Because understanding the Scripture is so foundational to every other spiritual discipline, we'll give our first full week to Bible study.

Though the Bible is a single book, it's also a collection of inspired writings. The canon of Scripture includes sixty-six books written over thousands of years by a variety of authors who lived in different places at different times, many of whom spoke different languages. While hundreds of stories are found within the books of the Bible, they all contribute to a single story: the grand narrative of God's creation, humanity's rebellion against Him, and His promised redemption of His people and our world through Jesus Christ. It is within this story that our own stories find meaning.

But meaning doesn't necessarily mean all about me—though I've often wished it were so. For the longest time, I approached the Bible looking for a word for the day or an answer to a pressing need. Should I say yes to this opportunity? Should I buy this house or that? The mountains or the beach for vacation? (Of course, the mountains.) While I believe God speaks to us in specific and sometimes downright unexplainable and supernatural ways, the Bible's meaning isn't up for grabs. There may be many ways to faithfully apply certain passages and the meaning of such passages may be layered. But when we read through the Bible, one thing is clear: God spoke, and we were meant to understand His message. We're not to make His message into what we want it to be or what our current culture thinks it should be or what social media posts say it means. This is enormously freeing.

So we must take care to interpret God's Word faithfully and accurately. This practice is sometimes referred to as *hermeneutics*. The term "describes the principles people use to understand what something means, to comprehend what a message—written, oral, or visual—is endeavoring to communicate."[1] Simply put, hermeneutics means faithfully interpreting what the Scriptures mean. To do this well, we ask certain questions: *Who is the author of the book we're studying (if known)? Who was it written to? When was it written? What was the culture like at the time?* Asking these questions to understand the Bible's original context can help us best know what it means in our own context. This is one of the

> When we read through the Bible, one thing is clear: God spoke, and we were meant to understand His message.

beautiful and timeless aspects of Scripture—understanding the original context doesn't lessen its meaning or application in our modern day; rather it bolsters it by opening our eyes to how others experienced the living God in their time.

Another important question to ask as we go along is: *What kind of literature is the book I'm studying?* For instance, the Old Testament includes books of Law, History, Poetry, Wisdom, and Prophets. The New Testament includes the Gospels, Acts, Epistles, and Revelation. We read each of them differently for the sake of interpreting them most accurately. If we take the metaphors of Psalms literally, we may find ourselves "making our beds in hell," which I really don't want anyone to try. If we're looking in the history books for a step-by-step approach to a healthy marriage, Solomon with his thousands of wives may not be the place to search. Knowing the Epistles are letters written by specific authors to specific individuals or churches helps us know that certain exhortations need to be contextualized—in our culture, for instance, greeting one another on a Sunday morning with a "holy kiss" might be a bit of a problem for pretty much . . . everyone.

While at first the contents of this introduction seem like a lot to consider, these principles will serve as aids and guardrails to make studying the Bible easier and clearer. We'll actually get to practice a little hermeneutics this week as we study what the Bible has to say about itself. We'll let Scripture interpret Scripture. We'll take into account the type of literature we're studying, depending on the passage. I'll employ a few simple tools like word dictionaries and commentaries to deepen our insight. And, most importantly, we'll look at every passage in its own context and within the larger context of Scripture. If you're overwhelmed, don't be!

The whole purpose of this week's study is to further acquaint you with God's Word and give you more tools in your belt to study it. This week isn't about how much you already know or how sharp your Bible skills are. It's about incorporating the tried and true practices of centuries of Christ-followers who found that certain disciplines created the best conditions for drawing close to our Savior. As we begin this adventure, we'll continually keep in mind that Bible study is not an end in itself. Listen to what Jesus said to some of the religious leaders of His day who knew the Scriptures inside and out, "You pore over the Scriptures because you think you have eternal life in them, and yet they testify about me. But you are not willing to come to me so that you may have life" (John 5:39-40). Ultimately, we practice the spiritual discipline of Bible study so we might know, love, and serve the Word made flesh, Jesus Christ. Whether you're a Bible study veteran or brand new to Scripture's pages, its treasures are inexhaustible.

A Speaking God

> I think a new world will arise out of the religious mists when we approach our Bible with the idea that it is not only a book which was once spoken, but a book which is *now speaking*.[2]

A. W. TOZER

Early this morning I took a walk around my neighborhood. Redbud trees line several of the streets, and they delight me so, especially when they bloom purple megaphones announcing to the world that spring is here. The strip of grass on the street-side of my sidewalk isn't wide enough for me to plant my own. Otherwise I'd have a row of waving redbuds greeting you upon arrival. That skinny sidewalk strip of grass is the one downside to my street.

Today on my walk I noticed a single languishing redbud in a row of thriving ones. The ones flanking it were several feet taller and vibrantly stretching upward; the flagging tree had a mere two branches growing mostly sideways. Cast in the shade of towering branches whose leaves blocked the sun, I realized the struggler was failing because it didn't have the light it needed to thrive. *Hmmm*, I thought to myself, *nature is hitting close to home today, and trees aren't supposed to meddle like that.* When other activities and busyness crowd out the time I need to hear from God, my growth is stunted, spiritually and otherwise. After all, God's Word is more glorious and penetrating than the sun, said the psalmist in Psalm 19. And when God's light transforms our hearts, I like to think we bloom like redbuds.

As we begin this session's homework on the study of God's Word, I can't help but start with a foundational passage in 2 Timothy.

Read 2 Timothy 3:14-17.

In Paul's letter to Timothy, he listed various things for which Scripture is useful or profitable (v. 16). What are they?

Who inspired or "breathed out" Scripture, and why should this cause us to prioritize studying the Bible (v. 16, ESV)?

The New Testament hadn't been compiled in Paul and Timothy's day. So when Paul referred to "all Scripture" (v. 16) what must he have been referring to?

What did Paul tell Timothy the "sacred Scriptures" (v. 15) are able to do?

So this is really interesting. When you consider that our New Testament didn't exist in Paul and Timothy's day, you realize the reference to the "sacred Scriptures" is a reference to the Old Testament. Yet here Paul attached the Old Testament to Jesus.

PERSONAL TAKE How do you think the Old Testament gives us wisdom for salvation through faith in Jesus?

This passage reminds us that studying the thirty-nine books of the Old Testament is as important as studying the twenty-seven in the New. This doesn't mean the Old Testament gives us everything we need to know, but understanding it is vital to fully grasping the messages and promises of the New Testament.

Today we'll look at a portion of the "sacred Scriptures" Timothy knew well, the ones Paul urged him to continue in. We'll begin in Exodus, the second book of the Bible. But first a little context: In the Book of Genesis, we see that God spoke to Adam and Eve, and later to Noah, Abraham, Isaac, Jacob, and Joseph. After God delivered Israel from Egypt, He spoke corporately to His chosen people through His servant Moses. As we consider the spiritual discipline of Bible study, beginning with God's instructions to Israel is an important and foundational place to start. (This is also a principle of hermeneutics: going to the early pages of Scripture to see what is said about a given matter.)

Read Exodus 19:1-6.

In this instance, what did God want the Israelites to do before anything else (v. 5)? (Circle the correct answer.)

Act   Listen   Worship   Repent

Sometimes we speak for trivial reasons, but God spoke because He had something vital to say to His people and wanted them to listen.

Read Exodus 20:1-2.

How did God reveal His personal nature to the Israelites before giving them the Ten Commandments?

What does this tell us about God's heart behind His commands?

If you thought the Ten Commandments were a lot to keep up with, God followed them up with an additional 603 laws for a grand total of 613—and I thought growing up in a strict private school was rough at times. The whole of these laws is referred to as *Torah*, the Hebrew word for *law*, and is contained in the first five books of the Old Testament, also known as the Pentateuch. (Note: When you see words in Scripture like law, precepts, instruction, or commands, more than likely the author is referring to the whole of the Torah.)

Sadly, the English translation *law* doesn't give us the most accurate impression of God's commands because it tends to steer our minds toward rules, prohibitions, and restrictions. However, the Hebrew word *Torah* is full of positive connotations about how God intended His people to thrive in the promised land.[3] Dr. John Sailhamer described it wonderfully, "What the man and woman lost in the Garden is now restored to them in the Torah, namely, *God's plan for their good*" (emphasis mine).[4] Did anyone need to hear that today? God's laws are for our benefit and blessing.

PERSONAL REFLECTION Describe a specific way that God's instruction in your life has been for your good, especially if that instruction went against the grain of your natural inclinations.

When we study God's Word and walk according to it, through the power of His Spirit, we're literally restoring the abundant life that was once ours in the garden. Sailhamer's words remind me that God's Word is not static but transformative in its power to change us (2 Cor. 5:17; Col 3:10)!

PERSONAL REFLECTION When you think of the Old Testament and God's Law in particular, do you have a positive or negative view? Explain.

How has what you've learned so far caused you to think differently?

Read Deuteronomy 4:1-14.

Deuteronomy begins with Moses addressing the people of Israel before they crossed the Jordan River into the promised land. He rehearsed the commands God gave them at Mount Sinai (Ex. 20), because at this point, the Israelites had spent the last forty years wandering in the wilderness as a result of their disobedience. As they prepared to enter the promised land, God had a lot to tell them through Moses.

What did Moses do with the commands God had given Israel (vv. 1,5,14)? (Circle the correct answer.)

Hid them   Passed them out   Recited them   Taught them

PERSONAL TAKE If it was important for Moses to teach God's Word to the people, what does that tell us we'll need along the way as we study Scripture?

PERSONAL REFLECTION Moses told the Israelites not to add or take away from God's commands (v. 2). How do you see these errors happening today?

Taking away from God's Word:

Adding to God's Word:

God's people were to listen to and follow God's words so that they might _____, _____, and _____ (v. 1).

What other reason did Moses give for keeping God's commands in verses 6-7?

What does verse 8 infer about the laws of Israel's surrounding nations?

It's natural to think of the Ten Commandments and the subsequent 603 laws as out of touch and antiquated. But we often don't realize how ahead of their time they were and to a large degree still are. While other ancient nations were lawless and hopelessly lived at the mercy of their false gods, God had given His people instruction for flourishing. The Law revealed how Israel could live at peace with God, each other, and even the foreigner in their midst.

As Israel was to stand apart from other nations, so we're to be set apart today. This doesn't mean we're to be distant from people who don't know Christ but rather distinct in how we live. When we live by God's Word, what differences do others see in our lives that might draw them to Jesus? Name some specific differences.

> Only be on your guard and diligently
> watch yourselves, so that you don't
> forget the things your eyes have seen
> and so that they don't *slip from your
> mind* as long as you live. Teach them to
> your children and your grandchildren.
>
> DEUTERONOMY 4:9 (EMPHASIS MINE)

Some translations use the word *mind* and others *heart*. That's because the Hebrew word encompasses all of our being. It's the "source of the life of the inner person . . . with a focus on feelings, thoughts, volition, and other areas of inner life."[5] Moses was clear: We're to know what God has told us, hold onto it with intent and care, and teach it to those coming behind us.

What excites you most about adding a regular discipline of Bible study to your life? What are your fears or concerns?

I can't wait to continue to trace the importance of God's Word throughout the pages of Scripture. I'm already looking forward to tomorrow where we'll take a look at the heart behind knowing the Word.

A Law of Love

Of one thing I am perfectly sure. God's story never ends with "ashes."[6]

ELISABETH ELLIOT

My friend Hollis was in the neighborhood and did an old fashioned drop in. I love when people spontaneously pop by (unless my house is a wreck or I'm still in my workout clothes and my hair is up in a clip!). Goodness, when did everything get so structured? Not surprisingly, I was perched on my front porch when Hollis pulled up. It's become my central office during the spring and summer, though I will say it's not a great setup if you're trying to focus. It seems that every twelve minutes or so I absolutely must water those barrels of roses in the back, steep another cup of tea, or drop everything for someone as remarkable as Hollis. Eighty-four years old and as charming as can be, Hollis reads the Scripture focus at our church on Sunday mornings. When the churches we separately attended merged together, he and I became fast friends, which led to him coaching me on how to swing a golf club (though that is an entirely different story).

Sitting lazily in outdoor chairs, we caught up in the afternoon air. I shared some uncertainties about the future, questions about things I have no control over. He crossed his legs and adjusted his sunglasses. Silence hung between us for a brief moment. "T and O," he finally said. I nodded my head and smiled. I'd learned his abbreviation for "trust and obey." "That's all you can do," he shrugged. At eighty-four, he's let that truth play out through bliss and trial. It was just the reminder I needed. And today it's the shorthand for much of what we'll be studying in the Book of Deuteronomy. While it doesn't have nearly the ring to it, for our purposes I'm changing his acronym to, "T and O because we L." I'll explain the L part in a moment.

Quick review from yesterday. What does the word *Torah* refer to?

Thoughtfully read Deuteronomy 6:1-9.

Verse 2 shows the correlation between fearing God (revering and respecting Him) and doing what He says. How does obeying God's Word reflect how much you revere Him?

In what place are God's words to dwell (v. 6)? How is this significant to your life today?

Verses 7-9 are gripping descriptions of how God's words are to thread through our daily lives. When my nieces and nephews are in my home, when I'm having dinner with friends, when I'm catching up with family, I want God's view of life and His guidance in my relationships to spill into every crevice of my day. Memorizing a list of rules doesn't accomplish this; having God's instructions live in my heart does.

Based on verse 3, what was promised if the Israelites obeyed God?

Deuteronomy 6:4-5 is known as the Shema, which literally means "Hear!" and is to be taken as a command. In ancient Israelite tradition, the Shema became a daily, recited prayer.[7]

Here's the CSB version:

> Listen, Israel: The Lord our God,
> the Lord is one. Love the Lord
> your God with all your heart,
> with all your soul, and with all
> your strength.

When you see *LORD* in small caps in the Old Testament, it's referring to Yahweh, the personal name by which God revealed Himself to His people

Why do you think it was important for the Israelites to know that their God was the one and only God of the universe? (Look back at Ex. 20:3-4 for clues.)

I want God's view of life and His guidance in my relationships to spill into every crevice of my day.

When I skim social media feeds or catch the daily headlines on my phone, I'm reminded that there are a lot of gods out there. To claim with certainty that you serve the one and only God of this universe is increasingly polarizing. Yet this is exactly who God reveals Himself to be in the Shema. Yahweh is the single, one true God.

What is the first word of the Shema, and why is it important?

The interesting thing about the word *listen* or *hear* in this context is that it's virtually synonymous with *obey*. The expectation was that tuning in to God's Word naturally meant you were preparing to respond to His leading. In other words, if you've really heard the one, true God, you'll obey Him. Put another way, if you say you've heard God but you don't actually obey Him, then you haven't really heard Him.[8]

> **PERSONAL REFLECTION** Is there something you've heard God say through His Word but haven't obeyed? If so, be honest with yourself and reflect on what's holding you back. Then briefly note your plan of action, such as removing a specific obstacle in the way of obedience or taking a step of obedience you've been neglecting.

According to Deuteronomy 6:5, with what three parts of our being are we to love the Lord our God?

1.

2.

3.

The word *heart* here "constitutes the mind or reason, which directs the rest of the person."[9] The word *soul* identifies "the life desire of the person . . . [it] is the element of the person that desires life, seeks it out, and experiences it."[10] The word *strength* is "tied closely with the physical strength of the person and so enables the performance of tasks prescribed by God's will."[11]

Based on these three definitions, write a specific way you love the Lord with your heart, soul, and strength beneath each word in the previous activity.

Many of you are familiar with Jesus' command to love the Lord with all our heart, soul, and mind (Matt. 22:37). What doesn't seem as well-known or obvious is why this would be at the heart of God's law for Israel.

Put another way, what does keeping 613 commands have to do with loving God? Or maybe I should ask, what does loving God have to do with obeying 613 commands? Any stabs?

As we've discovered today, to truly hear Him leads to obeying Him, which is the essence of what it means to love Him. "T and O because we L" stands for trust and obey because we love God. This may be one of the least sophisticated things I've ever written, but I hope it's memorable. Trusting and obeying God and His Word is rather incomplete—according to Deuteronomy 6:1-9—without it being attached to our loving the Lord. Bible knowledge combined with love results in changed hearts and lives. And isn't that what we so desperately want?

How does studying God's Word as a means to loving Him and others change your perspective of Bible study? Be specific. If studying the Bible has become mostly an academic pursuit for you, ask the Lord to inspire in you a love for Him and others.

I'm grateful that from the Bible's earliest pages we see God's instructions are meant for our flourishing and also as a means to a deeper relationship with Him. As we move through this session, we'll see how God's Word unfolds to us in and through the person of Jesus. I pray it compels us to T and O because we L. Don't judge me.

The Glory of the Word

The noise of the modern world makes us deaf to the voice of God, drowning out the one input we most need.[12]

JOHN MARK COMER

After spending the first two days looking at God's Word through His law, we'll now view it through song and poetry. (I can hear the applause.) When I was younger and in need of direction or a quick fix to a problem, I'd poke around the Book of Proverbs for an immediate road sign or answer. (I'm not saying this is a best practice.) I could readily apply a proverb to most any situation without too much expertise, which is one of the reasons I spent so much time in this book of wisdom. The psalms drew me in as well. When I was in high school, in the depths of despair over a season-ending basketball sprain or not being asked to prom until the bitter last minute, I would lament in Psalms. Its poetry gave wings to both my heartaches and hallelujahs, and Proverbs' wisdom grounded me in understanding. Both books are rich with history, theology, literary devices, and of course, inspired by the Holy Spirit.

In addition to Psalms and Proverbs, the poetic and wisdom books of the Bible include Job, Song of Solomon, and Ecclesiastes. Because portions of these writings are readily applicable to our modern lives, we tend to access them often. Today we're going to look at Psalm 19. It was one of my favorites growing up and has maintained that status into my adulthood. It describes the nature of God's Word and swells with poetry and metaphor. C. S. Lewis wrote this about Psalm 19: "I take this to be the greatest poem in the Psalter and one of the greatest lyrics in the world."[13]

Read Psalm 19. Note that the first six verses describe how God speaks to us through His creation and the rest of the psalm deals with how He speaks through His Word.

How does God "speak" to us through His creation (vv. 1-4)?

What two metaphors did David use to describe the sun in verses 4-5?

Verse 7 appears to abruptly jump from descriptions about the sun to a new section about God's Word. It would be natural to assume that these are two disconnected segments, but look closely at verse 6. It ends with the phrase, "nothing is hidden from its heat."

PERSONAL TAKE How might this transitional statement about the reach and power of the sun connect to what David said about the Word of God in verses 7-11?

Using trusted tools (commentaries, Bible dictionaries, concordances, and so forth) to study the Bible is particularly meaningful because they help us see the authors' intentions that aren't always obvious. Before studying this psalm, I would have thought the transition between the content in verse 6 about the sun and the content in verse 7 about God's Word was merely David changing gears to a brand new topic. But the *Word Biblical Commentary* tells me that the reality of there being nothing hidden from the sun's heat is a powerful analogy of God's Word: "The clause marks the transition between the two parts of the psalm and at the same time links them intimately together. Just as the sun dominates the daytime sky, so too does Torah dominate human life."[14] Okay! Now we're onto something that makes both parts of the psalm even more remarkable and meaningful!

Notice another subtle but important shift. In verse 1, David said creation declares the glory of God. But what different title did David use when referring to God in verses 7-9?

As we noted yesterday, LORD (with small caps) is the word for *Yahweh*, God's personal name given to the Israelites.

PERSONAL REFLECTION If creation declares the glory of God to all people, how does God's Word reveal His personal nature to His people? To use another of David's analogies, if the sun gives physical light to everyone, how does His Word give spiritual light to believers?

Verses 7-9 use different terms to describe the Torah (God's good Law for His people). Each term highlights a different facet of Torah, but together they form the diamond that is God's Word. Translations differ slightly, but I've listed and italicized the words used in the CSB.

VERSE 7

The *instruction* of the LORD is

What does it do?

The *testimony* of the LORD is

What does it do?

VERSE 8

The *precepts* of the LORD are

What do they do?

The *command* of the LORD is

What does it do?

VERSE 9

The *fear* of the LORD is

What does it do?

The *ordinances* of the LORD are

What are they more desirable
and sweeter than?

PERSONAL REFLECTION Which of these six statements about God's Word means the most to you, and why?

Just as the sun gives light and heat that is essential to survival and enjoyment, God's personal revelation through His Word is also indispensable to our lives. Without it, how would we know the Lord and His purposes for us? Where else would we discover that we're made in His image? And how would we know who Jesus is, what He did for us on the cross, and His desire to be in relationship with us?

Read verses 12-14 again.

> **PERSONAL TAKE** After writing about God's Word being a powerful light to our souls, why do you think David ended with confession and forgiveness?

Verse 14 says, "May the words of my mouth and the meditation of my heart be acceptable to you, LORD, my rock and my Redeemer."

This is one of my favorite verses to pray whether I'm beginning to pray or if I've run out of words at the end of my praying. It covers a thousand confessions and keeps me from as many future sins. If the words I speak and the thoughts and reflections of my heart are acceptable to the Lord, how can I sin against Him and His Word? Praise be to our rock and our Redeemer!

> **PERSONAL PRAYER** Write out a prayer based on verse 14. Add your personal pleas to it. To prompt you: What of your words need to change? What heart-reflections need to be different? What does "acceptable" (some versions say "pleasing") to the Lord look like? How is He your personal Lord, Rock, and Redeemer?

You're already more than halfway through our first session. I'm proud of you for sticking with the discipline of Bible study. Tomorrow, we'll look at God's Word through the pages of the New Testament, studying the perspective of James, the brother of Jesus. I think you'll find his understanding of the Word to be most practical and inviting. We're in this together.

Hearing and Doing

We have the presence and the promises of God. We are meant to march to that great music.[15]

AMY CARMICHAEL

One compelling aspect of writing this study is seeing each of the spiritual disciplines through the lenses of the Old and New Testaments. Today, we'll look at God's Word through the New, which incidentally is built upon the Old. If you needed more coffee for that opening thought, or heaven forbid, you don't drink coffee, let me give it to you straight—today is an exciting transition that will take on even more meaning after having studied God's Word in Deuteronomy and Psalms.

Read James 1:19-27.

> **What did James say is necessary before we receive God's Word? List everything he mentioned in verses 19-21.**

> **In what posture are we to receive the Word?**

> **What word did he use to describe the "word" in verse 21? (Circle the correct answer.)**

> *Implanted*   *Fruitful*   *Prolific*   *Cultivated*

When studying Scripture—especially when reflecting on it, which we'll get to later in our study—it's important to notice and contemplate individual words. For instance, James suggested the adverb *humbly* is significant to our being able to receive God's Word. If we come to Scripture with a prideful attitude, we won't be able to receive it in the way God intends. Similarly, notice the word *implanted*. You don't have to do a formal word search to ponder what that word means in this context.

> **PERSONAL TAKE** What does *implanted* tell us about how the Word of God works in our lives? List everything you can think of. (Questions to ask yourself: *Do planted things grow immediately? Do they require patience? Are strong roots and cultivating needed?* You get the idea.)

If you want to further study the meaning of a word or discover the other places it's found in Scripture, you'll need a concordance. (Go to *blueletterbible.org* or check out the resources listed on pp. 38–39.) *Implanted* means to be "marked by being deeply fixed or set within something."[16] It also means to "grow or spring up" or to be "inborn."[17] Interestingly, the only time the Greek word for *implanted* is used in the New Testament is here in James.[18] With that being the case, we're unable to see how other New Testament authors might have used the word. On the other hand, this onetime usage highlights James' desire to uniquely describe the way God's Word plants itself in our hearts.

What did James say the implanted word is able to do (v. 21)? (Note, the word here is most likely "referring to the word of the gospel."[19] In this instance, it's probably not a call for unbelievers to "accept the word" as much as it's for believers to "allow the word to influence them in all parts of their lives."[20]

In your own words, sum up James' instruction in verse 22.

Explain the illustration James used in verses 22-25 to describe a hearer of the Word who's not also a doer.

I can't think of a more natural response to being a hearer of the Word than being a doer as well. And yet somehow I always need to be reminded of James' instruction. If I'm not careful, I can substitute hearing, even studying the Word, for putting it into practice. Like reading a book on the importance of exercise but never moving or like making a salad and eating a pizza instead (I participated in this exercise yesterday), our knowledge and understanding of the Word counts for little if it doesn't express itself through corresponding action. Filling up on knowledge may give us a sense of righteousness, but it hasn't done its job if it doesn't bloom into obedient action.

James's illustration about looking in a mirror but then forgetting what one looks like is a brilliant image. How often do you look in the mirror without fluffing your hair or flossing a bit of spinach out of your teeth? When we obtain knowledge about the way we look by seeing our reflection in a mirror, we make a change. It's pretty simple.

What is the spiritual "mirror" James wanted us to intently look into? (Circle the correct answer.)

Our heart   Our feelings   The perfect law of freedom   Our friends

So far, James has referred to the Old Testament Scriptures as the Word, but here he referred to the Law in particular. While he may be using these words interchangeably, James had a keen interest in showing Jesus as the One who perfectly interprets and lives out the Law.21 On the first day of this session, we studied the Law in both Exodus and Deuteronomy. Today, we'll very briefly see how the Law takes on new meaning in the New Testament.

Read Matthew 5:17-18.

True/False: Jesus came to abolish the Law.

In Matthew 22:34-40, how did Jesus sum up the Old Testament Law?

PERSONAL TAKE How does loving God with our entire being and our neighbor as our self fulfill the entire Law?

James had the interesting privilege of being both an apostle and half-brother of Jesus. He was deeply acquainted with the teachings of Christ and therefore viewed God's law as one of love and freedom rather than a list of stringent rules that could only bring condemnation. He understood that when Christ fulfilled the law He empowered us to implement its commands from a new heart.

Look back at James 1:26-27. Here, James gives us some examples of what our lives will look like if we persevere in studying God's words while acting on what He tells us:

We'll control our _____. (Goodness, I need help with this every day).

We'll look after both _____ and _____. (We do this in different ways. Some adopt; some support; some serve; some give. We need to be doing something.)

We'll keep ourselves _____ from the world. (We'll desire holiness over the values of the current culture.)

James has so much more to say about what a doer of God's Word looks like. I encourage you to read the entire letter when you have the time. For the purpose of today's study, though, I want you to come away with how transformational and practical the words of Scripture are. It thrills my heart to write this because, frankly, I get so tired of my repetitive thoughts, my default ways of seeing the world, my go-to habits, my sin. I need a fresh word from the Word every day. Without the life and teachings of Jesus, it just would never occur to me to love my enemy or humble myself in a disagreement or stand up for justice when it might cost me or be generous when times are lean or simply say, "I'm sorry."

My land (as my grandmother used to say), I'm thankful I can look into the priceless law of liberty and then go do something about what I see. I'm ever grateful the Lord gives us an accurate mirror to look into, one that tells us the truth but doesn't leave us where we are. What a joy to know we are free to change! What a gift to be able to study the Bible so we can gain knowledge about Christ, be changed by what He teaches us, and impact the world around us. This is what the spiritual discipline of Bible study does for the person who, by God's grace, is willing to not just be a hearer but also a doer.

> **PERSONAL REFLECTION** What's one truth about God's Word that today's study has shown you?

DAY 5 — The Word Made Flesh

STUDY

The Word becomes flesh and walks among us, and so we have in our history not just the propositional Word of God, but the personal, lived-out Word of God, breathed by the Spirit, spoken by the Father, expressing fully His nature and purpose. God has spoken in His Son![22]

REUBEN WELCH

I grew up in a Christian home. Actually, I grew up in a pastor's home, so it was sort of double-Christian. From birth to high school graduation, I hardly ever missed a Sunday service. I could recite verses from the King James Version like it was my job, and I could knock your socks off in a sword drill. (For those who didn't grow up in a Bible church in the 80s, a sword drill is a game that tested your ability to quickly find a Scripture reference. Have no fear if you missed out—we've got apps for this. You're totally fine.) My point being, even with as much Bible study as I had as a child, you could have knocked me over with a feather when I first came across John 5:39-40.

Read John 5:39-40.

Who do the Scriptures testify about?

Place a checkmark by the correct statement:
- ☐ We have eternal life by knowing the Scriptures.
- ☐ We have eternal life by knowing Jesus.

While studying the Bible is essential to knowing who Christ is, it's possible to know what the Bible says without actually knowing Jesus. The religious leaders of Jesus' day knew the Old Testament better than anyone, yet they missed the One the Scriptures were all about. They missed Jesus. This is the last thing you and I want to have happen. So we'll close our session by studying the Word that was made flesh. If the spiritual discipline of Bible study has been a stiff and dry practice for you, I pray you'll gain a fresh perspective as we see Jesus as the embodiment of God's Word.

Read John 1:1-18.

From when was the Word (vv. 1-2)?

Fill in the blanks:

The Word was _____ God and the Word _____ God (v. 2).

What did the Word create (v. 3)?

Many of you may be familiar with this passage. You may have even memorized some of these verses about the Word. However, if we're honest with ourselves, these are not easy concepts to understand. What does it mean that the Word was at the beginning, that the Word was with God and was actually God Himself? How did it create, and how did it take on flesh and dwell among us? How is the Word a person?

If you look up the word *Word* in a concordance, you'll find the Greek word is *logos*. It simply means "word" or "message."[23] Because *logos* was a broad and widely used word in Jesus' time, the definition doesn't help us all that much. For a better understanding of what John is talking about, we need to go back to the Old Testament and see how its Hebrew equivalent, *dābār*, was used.[24]

Read Genesis 1:1-3,6,9,11.

How did God create? (Circle the correct answer.)

Thought   Prayed   Touched   Spoke

Read Psalm 33:6.

How were the heavens created?

> The heavens were made by the word of the LORD, and all the stars, by the breath of his mouth.
>
> Psalm 33:6

PERSONAL TAKE How do these Old Testament passages help you better understand Jesus' involvement in creation according to John 1:1-3?

We don't have time to look up the other ways God's Word was documented in the Old Testament, but His Word accomplished even beyond creation. God's Word came as revelation, deliverance, judgment, rescue, and wisdom.[25] I want you to see something else His Word accomplished—something especially dear to me.

Read Psalm 107:17-21.

What did God's Word do when He sent it forth (v. 20)?

When I think of all God's Word has done for me over the years, its healing power is at the top of the list. Nothing binds up wounded hearts, repairs broken thinking, or sometimes cures physical illness like His Word.

Throughout the Old Testament, God's Word created, revealed, delivered, judged, rescued, gave wisdom, and healed. Turn back to John 1 and read verse 14 again.

What did the Word do?

Who does John say is the Word that became flesh?

What was He full of? _____ and _____

> **PERSONAL REFLECTION** When you think of all the things God's Word accomplished in the Old Testament (see list above), describe what it means for the Word to have become flesh in Jesus.

The Word having "dwelt among us" is one of the most powerful phrases in all of Scripture (v. 14). The literal meaning is that the Word pitched His tabernacle among us.[26] The word *tabernacle* probably hasn't popped up in any of your recent texts or conversations—it's not a concept that has much meaning in today's culture. But if you were a first-century Jew, your mind would have immediately raced to the story of the Israelites wandering in the wilderness, found in the Book of Exodus.

Read Exodus 25:1-9.

According to verse 8, what was the purpose of building a tabernacle for God?

Though the presence of God dwelling among the Israelites was an astounding gift, often His glory was so great it was a consuming fire in which they couldn't draw near (Ex. 24:17). Even Moses couldn't enter the tabernacle when it was filled with God's glory (Ex. 40:34-35). And when the temple Solomon built was dedicated, the priests were kept from ministering there by God's glory (1 Kings 8:10-11).

> **PERSONAL TAKE** Imagine you're a first-century Jew hearing for the first time that God's Word was made flesh to dwell among you. You're just now understanding that His Word became a person, His very Son, to be with you. How would this have changed your perspective of God and His love for you?

In the fifth grade I had a teacher who banned the phrase "I don't get it" from the classroom. I was a repeat offender. She much preferred we incorporate the grammatically superior response, "I do not understand." Despite my misgivings at the time, this has served me well. But when I think about Jesus as the actual Word of God, the very expression of God Himself, the only thing that comes to mind is, "I don't get it!" (Sorry, Mrs. Shoaff.) And yet at the same time, I'm bowled over by the parts I do get. John, after having personally known and walked with Jesus, recognized that Jesus is God's ultimate expression of Himself![27] Jesus Christ, the Word that was from the beginning, the Word that creates, delivers, heals, and saves has dwelt among us, is accessible to us, is with us.

Read Hebrews 1:1-3.

By whom did God speak to the Old Testament fathers?

How does He speak to us today?

Through what is Jesus sustaining all things?

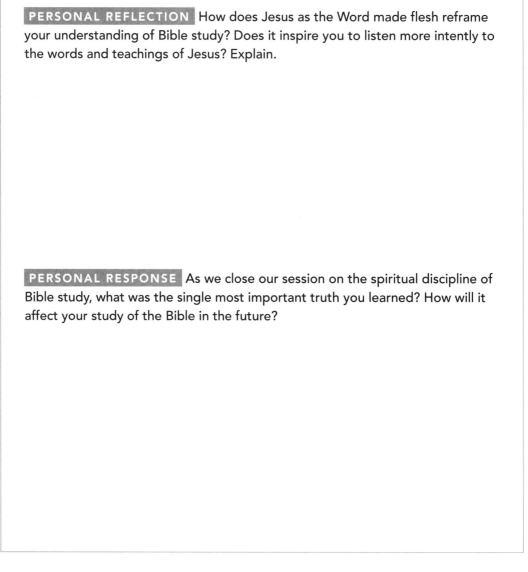

PERSONAL REFLECTION How does Jesus as the Word made flesh reframe your understanding of Bible study? Does it inspire you to listen more intently to the words and teachings of Jesus? Explain.

PERSONAL RESPONSE As we close our session on the spiritual discipline of Bible study, what was the single most important truth you learned? How will it affect your study of the Bible in the future?

Dear friends, I'm so grateful for your presence on this journey. The spiritual disciplines really are a road we travel because they lead us along paths of growth and understanding. As we commit time to each discipline, we're spending it with our Savior. I think of Mary of Bethany who chose to sit at the feet of Jesus and listen to what He said (Luke 10:38-42). Perhaps Mary understood even before John that she was in the presence of the Word made flesh and she best put down her pots and pans so she could partake of the portion that could never be taken from her (v. 42). I think that's what Bible study is. Spending time in the presence of Christ for that which nourishes us now and lasts into eternity.

Study

There are many different ways and means to study the Scripture. Here are a few tips to help you thrive in your study:

1. **Be consistent.** Make it a practice, hence the word *discipline.* But don't bite off more than you can reasonably chew. I tend to go overboard on everything, like the time I wanted to try my hand at gardening and built and planted five raised beds. It was too much too soon. Commit to what you can handle and then get after it.

2. **Give yourself grace.** If you miss a day, or days, don't get down on yourself. Pick back up where you left off. Remember, God isn't keeping a spiritual scorecard on how many days in a row you studied the Bible. He delights in our studying His Word because it's through His Word that we come to know Him more deeply. The Bible also reveals wisdom and knowledge about our lives, relationships, and what's important to the heart of Christ. Studying is for our blessing and benefit, not to curry favor with God or earn status with Him.

3. **Use available resources.** Choose a version of the Bible you enjoy reading. The CSB, ESV, and NIV are wonderful translations with easy-to-understand modern wording. The Message is an additional version that can be helpful alongside your main translation. I would encourage you to download the YouVersion Bible app. It gives you access to several versions of the Scripture, plus other helpful guides, like reading plans. Use Bible study tools such as concordances, dictionaries, and commentaries. Some of these you may want to purchase, such as Logos Bible Software (*logos.com*), but you can also find some of these tools for free online (*blueletterbible.org* and *biblegateway.com*).

4. **Always be sure to start with your own study of Scripture before you jump to using resources.** Ask the Spirit to speak to you about what the Word says before you see what others say about it. This takes restraint, especially in these days of being able to quickly Google a scholar's opinion or run to a word search. In all my years of being in God's Word, nothing sticks with me quite like the insights and truths I discover on my own through the power of the Holy Spirit.

For those just getting started (and those like me who can always use a refresher), here are some specific ways you can study the Scripture:

1. **Choose a Bible study that will lead you through a book of the Bible or a topic that can be traced throughout Scripture.** A study will keep you on track and will also guide you in your understanding not only of the passage you're studying but also how to study the Bible. We are blessed with countless resources that address every book in the Bible and just about every topic or theme there is to study in Scripture. Choose one that resonates with you. If you don't want to use a guided study, choose a book of the Bible to study on your own. (Check out Lifeway Women's Bible studies at *lifeway.com/women*.)

2. **Do a character study.** Choose an Old Testament character, like Noah, Abraham, Sarah, Joseph, Hannah, David, Daniel, and so forth. Or a New Testament character, like Peter, Paul, Mary, Elizabeth, or the women who followed Jesus in the Gospels. These are just a few of the many notable people in Scripture. And as you study certain individuals, always be looking for how God is working in their lives, how they respond to Him, and what you discover about His character.

3. **Read through the Bible in a year or two.** There are many reading plans, some of which guide you to read the Scripture cover to cover, while others are chronological. You can find Bible reading plans online. A daily reading plan helps with consistency—you know exactly what you need to do each day to finish in a specific amount of time. It also helps give you the big picture of Scripture. I like to use a journal when I'm reading through Scripture so I can write down anything that stands out to me.

WATCH SESSION TWO VIDEO

DISCUSSION QUESTIONS

What's something that really stood out to you in the video teaching?

How do the teachings of Scripture help us see the world as God sees it? To see things as they really are as opposed to how culture defines reality?

What is your history with the Bible? Was it a part of your growing up years? If so, how? If not, when did you first encounter the Scriptures?

How would you explain or describe the Bible to someone who knows nothing about it?

What are some recent things God has taught you through the Scriptures?

What does it mean for God to rebuke us through His Word, and how has He done that in your life?

How has God's Word corrected you and restored you to an upright position?

How has God used Scripture to nurture and train you?

What does it mean to be equipped for every good work? How is God accomplishing that in your life through His Word?

SESSION THREE

Pray

JOURNALING THE SESSION

Use this page throughout your session of study. We've given you some prompts, but feel free to write other thoughts and questions to help you learn and process the spiritual discipline of prayer.

PREPARING FOR THE SESSION

Before you start your work this session, journal some of your thoughts about the discipline of prayer. How have you practiced this discipline in the past? What has hindered your discipline of prayer? What do you hope to get out of this session?

DURING THE SESSION

What are some key things you're learning this session about the discipline of prayer?

REVIEWING THE SESSION

What are your biggest takeaways from this session, and how will you put them into practice?

Session Three Introduction

When I was a little girl, probably eleven or twelve years old, I got my hands on a serious Bible study on prayer. If I recall correctly, the study was set in a three-ring binder.

I told you, serious.

I was determined to become a better pray-er. I don't remember what happened to that study or if I even completed it. I just remember wanting to understand prayer better. To feel like my petitions and praises were tangible realities the Lord heard, as if they were individual butterflies making their way into His net. I wanted to experience the realness of prayer in some fashion, instead of so often feeling like my prayers were being released into thin air.

We use expressions like, "I feel like my prayers are hitting the ceiling," for a reason. When we're talking with a person face-to-face, we can see and hear them. But when we're talking to God, we often wonder what's happening up there—way above the ceiling. Does He hear us? And how do we hear Him back? Is prayer just a task we check off our list in the morning so we can get on with the real work? Or is it closer to what Oswald Chambers said, "Prayer does not fit us for the greater works; prayer *is* the greater work."[1]

I'm thrilled to spend a session with you on the spiritual discipline of prayer because regardless of all our questions, doubts, and the mysteries that surround prayer, we find in Scripture a God who summons us to seek Him, to converse with Him. And He intends for us to hear Him in return—according to the words of Jesus, His sheep know His voice (John 10:4). We can stand with the saints of old who believed in the effectiveness and power of prayer. Whether

it's Abraham, Sarah, Sarah's maidservant Hagar, Isaac, Isaac's servant, Rachel, Leah, Jacob, Joseph, Hannah, Samuel, David, Daniel, and the prophets in the Old Testament, or John, Peter, James, Anna, Paul, and the church in the New—God's people labored in prayer, and God responded!

Truth be told, prayer is one of the harder disciplines for me. I wake up, and I want to get cranking. I've got things to do. And tasks to accomplish. I need to text that person back; my pantry is a wreck, and I really should get those bags of rice organized; if I don't pull the weeds in the tomato beds, summer will be ruined. In his book *The Possibility of Prayer,* John Starke wrote, "The witness of Christian history is that the ambitious need quiet hearts. We need ancient paths for our modern, busy lives that teach us to be settled with God in an unsettling world."[2] Yes, the ambitious need to be quieted in the presence of the Lord. So do the anxious, those prone to controlling outcomes, the overachiever, and the one who needs a bit of prodding.

Finding a consistent place and consistent rhythm has helped me make progress in my prayer life since the days of the three-ring binder. I typically start my time with the Lord on my living room couch. But because it's nearly impossible for me to sit still in the mornings, I end up taking prayer walks through my house. If you happen to be strolling through my neighborhood and see me moving from room to room, talking to empty

> Finding a consistent place and consistent rhythm has helped me make progress in my prayer life since the days of the three-ring binder.

furniture, be not afraid. You have simply found me in prayer. And if you end up interacting with me later in the day, you'll be glad I began there.

For me, prayer helps me see the world as it really is—the way God sees it. I can get ratcheted up about all kinds of things; in prayer, God reminds me He is sovereign. I wake up in the morning with an agenda; in prayer, the Holy Spirit often reprioritizes my list. When I'm all worked up about the way someone is acting, prayer aids me in winning the spiritual battle, bidding me to forsake the one where flesh fights flesh. Prayer is the one activity that's effective in the midst of fear, grief, and impossible circumstances. Hannah must have known something about this when she poured out her heart to the Lord. (We'll look at Hannah's story later this session.)

The benefits of prayer are countless and immeasurable—too many butterflies to count in the net. But the greatest benefit is the relationship we gain in Christ. Once again Starke wrote, "Here's the basic assumption that the spiritual giants of Scripture and Christian history seem to have about prayer: Christ is personally and really present with us when we pray."[3] If this is true, how can we afford anything less than a consistent life of prayer? Yes, we'll need some discipline. But, mostly, we'll need the Holy Spirit, a regular rhythm, and a familiar chair in which to pray—or a place to walk prayer laps.

The God We Pray To

> Beloved disciple, seek above everything to be
> a person of prayer. Here is the highest exercise of
> your privilege as a branch of the Vine.[4]
>
> ANDREW MURRAY

When studying a biblical subject, especially one as vast as prayer, a good place to start is its earliest mention in the Bible. This is the approach we took last session when looking at the study of God's Word. It seems the curtain doesn't open up on prayer quite as dramatically as it does the Law. Moses didn't descend a blazing mountain with ten ways to pray, thus saith the Lord. In fact, prayer isn't even listed as one of the Ten Commandments. I suppose this is because people were praying before the Ten were given.

Prayer creeps onto the scene without much ado. The day it was birthed—I'm not sure. But in Genesis 1:26-28, we discover that God created man and woman in His image, blessed them, and delighted to give them rule over His creation. How did He issue this blessing? He spoke to them. Maybe this is why there was no grand prayer announcement. When a relational God creates humans in His image, the most natural thing in the world is that He would speak to us and we to Him. No stone tablets needed for this to be known.

Read Genesis 4:25-26.

What did people begin to do around this time?

PERSONAL TAKE The name *Enosh* means "weakness."[5] I doubt this is coincidence. How does the meaning of Enosh's name possibly relate to the people beginning to pray?

An important theological note here: The lineage from Adam to Noah runs through Seth, not Cain. Genesis 5 documents this lineage. The fact that the people in and around Seth's family began to call on the name of the Lord sets them apart from Cain's descendants and Noah's contemporaries.[6] Prayer becomes a marker of God's people.

Read Deuteronomy 4:4-8.

> Moses spoke these words to Israel as they prepared to enter the promised land many years after Seth and Enosh. According to verse 7, what continued to set Israel apart?

I want to spend the rest of today's study looking at the prayers of a woman named Hannah. Her prayers are some of my favorites in all of Scripture. And since she lived quite early in Israel's story, she offers a solid foundation for our study on prayer. Hannah made famous the idea of pouring out one's heart to the Lord. For context, Hannah lived during a significant transition in Israel's history—the period between the judges ruling Israel and Israel's monarchy. Her son, Samuel, would play a vital role in that transition, a reality that's even more significant when you read Hannah's story.

Read 1 Samuel 1:1-18.

> What was the cause of Hannah's pain (v. 6)?

> How long did Hannah's suffering persist (v. 7)?

> Where did Hannah pray with many tears (vv. 9-10)?

> **PERSONAL REFLECTION** Verse 10 tells us that Hannah prayed to the Lord out of her deep anguish. This tells us that Hannah believed the Lord was powerful enough and cared enough to change her circumstances. When you approach God in prayer, which do you struggle with believing the most and why—that He's powerful enough or that He cares for you enough?

What name did Hannah call God (v. 11)?

Hannah is the first person recorded in Scripture to use the name *LORD of Armies* (some translations say *LORD of Hosts* or *LORD Almighty*). This name of God tells us so much about who He is and who Hannah perceived Him to be. The title exalts the Lord as unmatched in His power and authority over the heavenly and earthly realms. While Eli, the not so fabulous priest, referred to the Lord by the more general name of *Elohim* (v. 17), Hannah saw God as all-powerful![7]

Hannah specifically asked the Lord to take notice of her affliction, to remember her, and not forget her. (The idea of God remembering someone in the Old Testament isn't the opposite of forgetting them. Rather, it means to take action and is often in keeping with His redemptive work in history.)[8] Keep in mind that few in that day would have thought Hannah an obvious candidate to be communing with and asking miraculous things of the Lord. This was partly because she was a woman and women didn't typically figure into the top of religious society, and partly because she was unable to conceive. Without a son to carry on her husband's family name, she had little standing in society and in her faith community. Don't miss how significant it is that Hannah not only saw God for all the authority and power He possesses, but also that she felt welcome to share with Him her deepest concerns.

> **PERSONAL REFLECTION** How does God's title *LORD of Armies* give you the courage to pray bigger and bolder prayers?

Look back at verses 15-16. Hannah referenced having poured out her heart to the Lord. How does her passion reveal the places where you're withholding your own pain from the Lord, trying to handle your circumstances apart from Him?

Notice in verse 18 that after Hannah prayed and talked with Eli the priest, she ate. This isn't a reference to Hannah grabbing a sandwich because it was past dinnertime. Hannah was choosing to participate in the feast at Shiloh with her family and friends, something she hadn't done earlier (v. 7). This is really significant.

PERSONAL TAKE Hannah had yet to receive her request from the Lord. But we notice a change in her spirit as evidenced by her eating with the community and her face no longer being sad. How do you think prayer transformed her even though her circumstances had yet to change?

Continue reading 1 Samuel 1:19-20,27.

What did Hannah and her husband do the next morning (v. 19)?

What did Hannah name her son, and why (v. 20)?

PERSONAL REFLECTION Hannah participated in the feast at Shiloh, and she worshiped in the Lord's house before God answered her prayers for a son. Do you have a bold, desperate request you're asking of God? Write down one way you can keep participating with God's people and one way you can worship while you wait on the Lord for your heart's desire.

God responded to Hannah's prayer and performed a miracle within her. The LORD Almighty gave Hannah one of the most remarkable sons in all of Israel's history, but not before many years of barrenness and grief. Even in the middle of her pain, Hannah never ceased the spiritual discipline of annually journeying to the tabernacle at Shiloh and worshiping, entrusting the Lord with her deepest desire.

Let's close by looking at Hannah's prayer of thanksgiving and praise.

Read 1 Samuel 2:1-10.

> **PERSONAL REFLECTION** What is the most meaningful phrase to you in Hannah's prayer at this season of your life, and why?

The line that gets me every time is, "It is not by strength that one prevails," (v. 9, NIV). This resonates with me because I have tried so earnestly to achieve in my own power only to discover how limited my supply truly is. At Justice & Mercy International's last jungle pastors conference in the Amazon, my dad and I sat with Manoel, one of our favorite Amazonian pastors. Pastor Manoel was explaining his struggle to get people in his village to church. Eventually, he threw up his hands, smiling as broad as the Amazon River itself, and exclaimed in Portuguese, "I am filled with incapacity!" My dad and I laugh about this moment every time we rehearse it because to be full of lack is an oxymoron, yet nothing felt truer to our understanding of ourselves. How we all need the Lord the way Hannah and Pastor Manoel need Him.

Who did Hannah's heart rejoice in (v. 1)?

What did Hannah say about Samuel in her prayer? (Hint: this is a bit of a trick question.)

I'm continually moved by the fact that Hannah never mentioned Samuel by name in her prayer. This absence certainly isn't because Samuel was anything less than all she could have ever hoped for. I have to believe that in pouring out her heart to the Lord, in worshiping Him in the midst of her suffering, she ultimately found the Blesser to be far grander than the blessing.

I once heard Beth Moore say something that really struck me: *Prayer is about access more than answers* (Eph. 2:18).[9]

If that is our perspective, all our prayers are "successful" because we will have encountered God regardless of His answer.

> **PERSONAL REFLECTION** What stood out most to you today about prayer, and why?

The focus of our prayers is often on the answers we're seeking, the much-desired change in our circumstances. But what if our focus is the Lord of Armies? What if we believed what Hannah believed about the Lord? That the God we pray to is far above every power and authority. That we have astounding access to pour out our hearts before Him.

Yes, we practice the spiritual discipline of prayer because prayer changes things. But we mostly practice it because it is through prayer that we commune with the living God, and He changes us.

It is through prayer that we commune with the living God.

Aligning Our Wills

> The essential difference between pharisaic, pagan and Christian praying lies in the kind of God we pray to.[10]

JOHN STOTT

One of my friends is an accomplished music producer in Nashville. I think of him as one of the best in the business, which is saying a lot in a town also known as Music City. One day I asked him if he mixes his own records (engineers the final sound). His answer surprised me. He almost always hires someone else to mix his projects. "When it comes to the sonic quality I'm after," he explained, "I have difficulty locating 'true north.'" I think he's overly critical of himself, but his sentiment stayed with me. Sometimes I'm not sure if my prayers are pointed true north. I may know the knobs to twist and the buttons to push, but how do I know if I'm praying "the right way"?

Yesterday, we learned from the earliest pages of Scripture how foundational and unique a gift that prayer is to God's people. The ability to commune with God set Israel apart from other nations, and it sets apart Christ-followers today. We could turn to so many places in the Bible to learn more about prayer, but I can't help but go to the place where Jesus spoke about it Himself. When we pray the way Jesus taught us to pray, we can be assured our prayers are headed true north.

Read Luke 11:1-4.

What did Jesus' disciple request that He teach them (v. 1)?

PERSONAL TAKE When it comes to prayer, what does this basic question tell us we need?

Read Matthew 6:5-8. These verses lead up to the Lord's Prayer (sometimes called the Disciples' Prayer). I want to begin with them since they shed light on the prayer Jesus taught us to pray.

The hypocrites Jesus referred to were some of the religious leaders (Pharisees) of the day. What motivated them when they prayed?

PERSONAL TAKE In contrast to the hypocrites, why do you think Jesus instructed His disciples to pray in secret?

Look back at verses 7-8.

In contrast to the Jewish religious leaders who prayed to the one, true God but for the wrong reasons, Jesus also referenced the pagan Gentiles who prayed to a myriad of gods. Why are we not to pray like the Gentiles?

Jesus told His disciples not to pray like the Jewish hypocrites because their motives were selfish. But He also told His disciples not to pray like the Gentiles, either, who hoped to manipulate the gods by their relentless babbling. Jesus taught that our prayers are to look different from the Gentiles' prayers because our God is different!

According to verse 8, how is God our Father different from the Gentiles' pagan gods?

Does verse 8 make you wonder why you should bother praying if your heavenly Father already knows what you need? I asked this question often, until one day it dawned on me—*Would I rather my heavenly Father not know what I need?* Can you imagine the conversations we'd have with Him? We pray for a job, and then God, wringing His hands, responds, "If only you'd told Me this earlier! There was this amazing position a few months ago, but I let it go by because I didn't know you needed one." It doesn't take long to see how ridiculous praying to a non-omniscient God would be. This doesn't answer all our questions about why we're to pray for what God knows we need, but it gives us confidence that He sees the beginning from the end, never misses a heart's longing, and is already prepared with necessary provisions because He's been out in front of us from eternity.

The fact that He knows what we need is precisely what sets him apart from the Greek gods of the first century who were distant, fickle, and unpredictable. We may tend to take for granted the idea that God is personal and caring, but that wasn't how the Greeks of Jesus' day, or the people of the Ancient Near East in Hannah's day, thought about their gods. That God in the Old Testament created men and women in His image to be in relationship with Him and that Jesus portrayed God as a loving Father in the New Testament went against the grain of popular belief in those eras.

> **PERSONAL REFLECTION** What does Jesus' teaching in Matthew 6:5-8 tell us about the nature and character of our God? How does this insight encourage or challenge the way you pray?

Read the Lord's Prayer from Matthew 6:9-13 (CSB) below. For continuity we'll answer questions based on this translation.

> [9]Therefore, you should pray like this:
> "Our Father in heaven,
> your name be honored as holy.
> [10] Your kingdom come.
> Your will be done
> on earth as it is in heaven.
> [11]Give us today our daily bread.
> [12]And forgive us our debts,
> as we also have forgiven our debtors.
> [13]And do not bring us into temptation,
> but deliver us from the evil one."

Matthew used the phrase "Father in heaven" (and "heavenly Father") twenty times in his Gospel, a distinctly Matthean theme he was passionate about making known. The term "Father in heaven" is so familiar to us that we often don't give it a second thought.[11] But this idea was somewhat new in the disciples' day. Jesus' arrival brought a fresh understanding of God's nature—Almighty God in heaven as our Father.[12]

How does the term *Father in heaven* compare and contrast with *LORD of Armies*, the name of God we studied yesterday?

Hold your place in Matthew 6 and turn to Matthew 7:9-11.

According to Jesus, what is our heavenly Father like and not like?

Jesus knew the concept of a loving heavenly Father is difficult to grasp for those who have painful relationships with their earthly fathers. I believe this is one of the reasons why Jesus told us that our Father in heaven is altogether good and trustworthy. He will not withhold from us. But Jesus also showed us something additional: He will not deceive us. No good earthly father, when his child asks for a loaf of bread, would trick the child with a lookalike stone. Neither would he try to fool his child by giving an eel-like snake instead of a fish.[13] If the earthly father desires to give good gifts to his children, how much more does our heavenly Father long to give us good gifts? (Luke 11:13 says He gives the Holy Spirit.)

PERSONAL REFLECTION How does Jesus' revelation of God as a loving Father encourage you to draw near to Him?

Now we're ready to look at the Lord's Prayer in Matthew 6:9. Keep in mind that this is a pattern for praying. It's not a rote prayer we're to parrot back to the Lord; rather, it gives us a model to draw from and incorporate into our own prayers.

He sees the beginning from the end, never misses a heart's longing, and is already prepared with necessary provisions.

From verses 9-11, complete the following:

Your name _____.

Your kingdom _____.

Your will _____.

PERSONAL TAKE Why do you think Jesus told us to start with the "Yours" before we get to the "ours"?

Praying about God's name, kingdom, and will are slightly different variations of the same petition.[14] Each of them helps align our wills with the Lord's in prayer, assuring we're headed true north. Consider each below:

God's Name: God's name isn't just about His title. It refers to His person, character, and authority.[15] When we pray for His name to be hallowed, or set apart as holy, we're praying that every part of Him, His entire being, character, and nature be exalted.

Kingdom of God: Matthew used the phrase thirty-two times in his Gospel! The meaning of God's kingdom is a big topic and not easily defined in limited space. In short, it is about God's perfect reign and rule. Though the kingdom of heaven has come to earth through the person of Jesus, it has yet to come in full. This is why we pray expectantly that the kingdom of heaven would rule completely on earth.

God's Will: This refers to the "redemptive and moral intent of God for this world and for God's people."[16] When we pray for God's will, we're praying for Him to act.[17] We're also agreeing to work in accordance with His purposes so we can be active participants in what He's accomplishing on earth.

Look at the end of verse 10. Fill out the key phrase that pulls these three concepts together: "on _____ as it is in _____."

In heaven, God's holy name is fully honored. In heaven, His kingdom is fully established. In heaven, His will is fully executed. Jesus told us to pray that everything that's true in heaven would also be true on earth. The kingdom coming to us transforms our broken, sinful, and groaning world in the here and now. Its inauguration impacts our families, our churches, and communities.

PERSONAL REFLECTION In what specific area of your life do you want to see God's name honored, His kingdom ruling, or His will done in the same way these are being accomplished in heaven? In short, where do you want God's rule to intersect your life? Write it down and commit to praying over this throughout our study.

How often do we begin our prayers by aligning our will with God's? So often we complain that our prayers aren't changing anything or that God isn't answering. But have we stopped long enough to make sure that what we want is what He wants? That what we're praying is what He wills? Our prayers will never be perfectly stated, nor is that even the goal. But our prayers will certainly be more effective when we begin with God's renown.

God's renown, God's kingdom, and God's sovereign will is our true north. When we begin our prayers the way Jesus taught, we know we're headed in the right direction. Our request for daily needs that follow, the complex situations we need wisdom for, and the petitions we plead for others and ourselves all find their proper places when we've first esteemed the King of the kingdom.

PERSONAL PRAYER Close today in prayer, beginning by aligning your will with God's. Pray Matthew 6:9-10 and make it your own.

Tomorrow we'll focus on the second half of the Lord's Prayer. If the first half emphasizes the glory and rule of our God, the second half emphasizes our physical and relational needs as humans. While heaven and earth are separate, the Lord's Prayer sets our hope on the day when God's kingdom in heaven will fully come to earth and the two will be made one.

DAY 3

PRAY

Aligning Our Wants

> For most of us, the problem is not that we are too eager to ask for the wrong things. The problem is that we are not eager enough to ask for the right things.[18]

N. T. WRIGHT

Throughout his Gospel, Matthew talked about the difference between heaven and earth.

Jonathan Pennington said, "Matthew is urging upon us the sense that there is a great disjunction between heaven and earth, between God's way of doing things and ours."[19] Can we please stop for a moment and acknowledge that, on most days, our way of doing things is quite different than God's? This is simply an ever-present struggle for me. I am forever having to reorient my will and desires to His. In the words of the great hymn, "prone to wander, Lord, I feel it, prone to leave the God I love."[20]

This is why I need to begin my day in prayer, realigning myself with God's renown, His kingdom agenda, and His will. Praying that God's kingdom will work its reality in my life is like laying my human nature on the chiropractor's table and getting a spiritual adjustment. A crack here, a this-won't-hurt-too-bad there, and I'm back in alignment with the heart of Christ. Unfortunately, I do find that I tend to slip out of spiritual alignment faster than most. Which is one of the reasons I'm looking forward to reflecting on the second half of the Lord's Prayer with you. It's a glorious invitation to fully depend upon our heavenly Father.

Read Matthew 6:9-13.

> Look back at verse 11. If we consider verse 11 as starting the second half of the prayer, how does the focus shift from the first half to the second?

Looking at verses 11-13, complete the following:

Give us _____.

Forgive us _____.

Do not bring us _____.

Deliver us _____.

The Lord knows we have daily needs that must be met and issues that come up in our relationships that require forgiveness, as well as trials and suffering that can tempt us to turn away from Him.

PERSONAL REFLECTION Before we break down the elements of the "ours," which petition in verses 11-13 is most significant to you right now, and why?

Daily Bread: Some of the early church fathers, such as Tertullian, Cyprian, and Augustine, found the practical request of daily bread to be too great a leap from the petitions relating to God's glory that came before it.[21] In other words, they didn't think our mundane needs fit alongside the prayers about God's greatness and kingdom. So they allegorized bread to mean either the Word of God or the Lord's Supper.

Two of the most renowned Reformers, Calvin and Luther, thought just the opposite. They interpreted daily bread literally, including anything that pertained to our basic needs and provisions. In this instance, I agree with the Reformers, and many others, who see the petition for daily bread as Jesus' way of acknowledging how important our physical needs are to our heavenly Father.[22] To me, the vast leap between the glory of God and our physical need for sustenance only further emphasizes God's loving condescendence toward us in the person of Jesus.

Read Exodus 16:1-5. This account takes place shortly after the Israelites left the bondage of Egypt on their way to the promised land. They struggled in the in-between place of the wilderness, complaining to Moses about their sparse provisions.

What specifically did God provide for the Israelites, and how often did He provide it?

For the Jewish audience of Jesus' day, a prayer for daily bread would have brought to mind the manna God provided for the Israelites in the wilderness. The strong connection to Exodus 16 and other emphases on our heavenly Father meeting our physical needs in Matthew further reinforces the thought that "daily bread" is directly related to God's care for our physical needs.

PERSONAL REFLECTION How does praying for God to meet your basic needs put you in a posture of dependence on your heavenly Father? Why is this good?

Forgive us our debts: Luke's Gospel uses the word *sins* instead of *debts* (Luke 11:4), but basically the words are used in the same way. However, Matthew's terminology gives us a picture of how our sin makes us debtors to God, carrying a debt we cannot possibly repay. This language gives us a slightly different perspective: Our debt before God is forgiven because Christ paid our debt on the cross.

Back to Matthew 6:12. Just as food is indispensable to our bodies for life and health, how is God's forgiveness toward us essential to our souls? Reflect on how significant it is that daily bread and forgiveness are placed side by side in this passage.

> When I don't seek God's forgiveness as a regular part of my prayers, I not only minimize my sin, I unintentionally minimize the richness of His mercy and grace in my life.

When I don't seek God's forgiveness as a regular part of my prayers, I not only minimize my sin, I unintentionally minimize the richness of His mercy and grace in my life. God's once and for all forgiveness of sin for salvation, through the death and resurrection of Christ, was rightly emphasized in the Christian tradition I grew up in. The downside is that I sometimes falsely assumed my daily, "minor-ish" sins didn't matter that much. They were covered. And while they are covered in the sense that I've been justified (made righteous) by faith in Christ, I have an ongoing need to receive His generous forgiveness for the sins I commit daily.

Lead us not into temptation; deliver us from evil: The Book of James helps us determine what this section of the Lord's Prayer means.

According to James 1:13-15, what does James tell us God will never do?

According to James 1:2-4,12 what is beneficial to our faith?

We must read verse 13 of the Lord's Prayer in the light of knowing God doesn't tempt us to sin, and that trials and hardship can strengthen our faith and deepen our relationship with Jesus. John Stott offered this possible interpretation of that verse: "Do not allow us so to be led into temptation that it overwhelms us, but rescue us from the evil one."[23] I think because we know our own weakness and tendency to sin, we ask our Father to keep us from temptation that would overwhelm us or take us under. Along those lines, we ask Him to deliver us from the sway of the evil one.

PERSONAL REFLECTION Without revisiting past sin in your life and without feeling like you have to be overly detailed, how would you finish this two-part prayer based on what you know about yourself?

Heavenly Father, lead me not into . . .

Heavenly Father, deliver me from the evil one and his scheme of . . .

Read Matthew 6:12,14-15. Here, Jesus gave us a bit more commentary on the importance of forgiving others.

According to verses 12,14-15, why is forgiving others so essential to our prayer life and our relationship with our heavenly Father?

At first glance, verse 15 can seem as if Jesus was teaching that God's forgiveness toward us is earned by us forgiving others. It's more likely He was expressing that if we've truly experienced God's lavish forgiveness in our lives, we will desire to extend forgiveness to others—even if we have to fight our human nature in the process to do so.[24] And when Jesus said in verse 12, "as we also have forgiven our debtors," He was assuming we are in the regular habit of forgiving those who have sinned against us. Since God's personal forgiveness toward us as individuals is so gracious and relational, we should forgive others in the same spirit.

Jesus expounded upon this idea in Matthew 18:21-35. Read this parable.

Look back at verse 27. In what specific ways did the master in the parable show compassion to his servant?

PERSONAL TAKE What is so astonishing about this parable?

Studying this element of the Lord's Prayer about forgiving others has brought timely conviction to my heart. I've been harboring unforgiveness toward someone, hardly aware of how much it has affected my prayers, even my relationships. I require the patience of so many, and yet I have been short with this person. I have held a grudge. I guess I've been withholding forgiveness because it feels justifiable to do so. That's the funny thing about unforgiveness; you can almost always make a solid case for it. That is, until you come up against your own sin. Your own debt. And then remember the compassion of Christ and how He forgave that debt in full.

Studying this passage reminds me that unforgiveness obstructs my prayers because it minimizes my acknowledgment of the compassion and grace Jesus has shown me. Forgiving others is so essential to receiving our own forgiveness because anything less reveals we don't understand how much we've been forgiven and how deep God's compassion is for us.

PERSONAL REFLECTION How does God's forgiveness toward you inspire you to forgive others?

PERSONAL PRAYER Is there anyone you need to forgive? If so, do that now and confess your own need for God's forgiveness.

In the second half of the Lord's Prayer, we're reminded that our physical needs, as well as our spiritual and relational needs, matter to God. I don't think the Lord's Prayer was meant to be exhaustive. As mentioned earlier, Jesus gave us this prayer as an example. We should pray about specific people, situations, and desires that aren't contained in this short section of Scripture, yet the Lord's Prayer will always serve as home base. If we have our daily provisions, a right relationship with God, and a right relationship with others, doesn't this just about cover all our bases? And isn't this as much as any of us could ask for?

The Ways We Pray

The first prerequisite of discipleship is being with Jesus.[25]

JAMES R. EDWARDS

I have the best physical therapist in Nashville. She is extremely gifted and perennially perky—she also takes an unreasonable amount of joy in driving her elbow into the most desperate and ailing parts of my body. Gina claims she does this to "loosen things up." I find this most suspect. If there's anything I've learned in PT over the years, it's that you straighten before you strengthen. Gina always checks my alignment first, making sure that my bones and ligaments and muscles are correctly moving and firing and whatever else they're supposed to do—I got a D+ in Human Anatomy, true story—before we start my array of exercises. If I approach my exercises with a crooked posture, I will only reinforce that position. Thankfully, the reverse is also true.

So far this session we've looked at Hannah's prayers and the Lord's Prayer. I chose those prayers because they help ensure we're approaching prayer with the correct posture. This doesn't mean perfectly, just rightly. We solidified the fact that God is all-powerful and deeply caring. We determined that our ability to come and dialogue with Him in prayer is a definitive marker of God's people—this idea was not assumed in the Ancient Near East or in the Greco-Roman world. We were reminded that one of the purposes of prayer is to change us and align our will with God's. We pray most effectively when we esteem our heavenly Father and ask for His rule and reign to inhabit our lives. We also learned that our Father longs to meet our needs and give us good gifts, not the least of which is the indwelling of the Holy Spirit.

> **PERSONAL REFLECTION** What is something new you've learned this session that's helped correct your posture of prayer?

Today we'll cover three basic types of prayer: adoration, petition, and thanksgiving. And tomorrow we'll cover a fourth, confession.

PRAYER OF ADORATION

We will never go wrong by beginning our times of prayer with praise and adoration. (See Ps. 100:4 and Matt. 6:9-10.) In Paul's letter to the Colossians, he included a hymn about Christ. I've recently used it as a springboard for my own prayers of praise as I reflect on the language Paul used about our Savior.

Read Colossians 1:15-20.

Make a list of Christ's attributes and actions in this hymn.

PERSONAL REFLECTION Look back at your list. Which attribute or action of Christ means the most to you right now, and why?

PERSONAL PRAYER Pray through this hymn, praising and adoring Jesus for who He is and what He's done.

Praying through this hymn helps me put my life's hopes and concerns in perspective. When I think about Jesus having first place in everything, I'm relieved that I don't have to strive to get out in front. Jesus is number one in all things. It's all about Him. When I'm burdened by unsolvable, complicated problems, Colossians 1:17 reminds me that Christ is before all things—meaning nothing has taken Him by surprise. Nothing confuses or confounds Him. You can see how each of these truths naturally gives rise to praise. Scripture is the best place to go when looking for prayer prompts.

What is one truth about Christ from this passage that helps put something in your own life in perspective?

PRAYER OF PETITION AND INTERCESSION

To petition the Lord is simply to ask Him for something. We can petition for ourselves, or others, which is also known as intercessory prayer. Petition is a large category that would encompass our prayers for guidance, wisdom, healing, help, rescue, salvation, a change of circumstances, and so forth.

Turn back a page or two in your Bible and read Philippians 4:6-7.

What did Paul invite us to do instead of succumbing to worry?

What specifically are we to present to God?

And in what attitude should we present our requests? Why do you think this is important? (We'll talk more about this shortly.)

PERSONAL RESPONSE Write down three requests that you want to regularly bring before the Lord throughout this study. Record them below.

Read Ephesians 1:15-23. In his letter to the church at Ephesus, Paul recorded a prayer of intercession. I often use this as a guide when praying for myself or others.

What did Paul never stop doing when he prayed for the believers in Ephesus (v. 16)?

List in bullet point format the requests that Paul made for his friends in verses 17-19. The bullet points help me break down the elements of his prayer. I've listed the first one to help you get started.

- *That God would give them the spirit of wisdom and revelation in the knowledge of Christ*

-

-

-

Read Ephesians 3:14-21.

This is another one of my favorite intercessory prayers I pray for others and for myself. As with the previous activity, list the aspects of this prayer. Again, I've filled in the first one for you. I also italicized "inner being" because that phrase always stands out to me. As much as I would love to be a tad more physically fit, I desperately want that inner strength Paul spoke of. So if something stands out to you in this prayer, underline or circle it.

- *That God would strengthen them with power in their inner being through His Spirit*

-

-

-

-

-

Colossians 1:9-14 is another one of my favorite intercessory prayers you can use to pray for yourself or someone you love. This is a bonus reference. You're welcome.

PERSONAL REFLECTION What keeps you from regularly petitioning for yourself and/or interceding for others?

PERSONAL PRAYER God wants us to bring before Him every situation that concerns us. Spend a few minutes praying over the requests you wrote down earlier.

PRAYER OF THANKSGIVING

(As we briefly look at giving thanks in prayer, know we'll spend a whole day on this discipline when we get to Session Four on Worship.)

In Luke 17, Jesus healed ten lepers but only one returned to thank Him. Incidentally, to thank someone who helped you in ancient Jewish culture was to recognize you had nothing to repay that person with. In returning to Jesus, the healed leper was not only thanking Him but also acknowledging his inability to give Him anything in return (Luke 17:11-19).[26] How great is that kind of thanks!

This month marks twenty years of me living in Nashville. It would be easy to let the month pass without thanksgiving or gratitude—because, like the nine lepers, the busyness of life carries on. But this morning I paused to journal and pray, to thank God and reflect on His unflagging faithfulness and goodness to me. I remembered that returning to Christ in thanksgiving isn't an ancillary activity but one that stokes the fires of remembrance, warming our hearts by His past faithfulness.

Read 1 Thessalonians 5:16-18.

True/False: We're to give thanks in all circumstances, even when our circumstances are hard.

Read Hebrews 12:28-29.

Why did the author of Hebrews tell us we can be thankful?

Read Colossians 2:6-7.

If we're rooted and built up in the person of Jesus, what will naturally overflow in us?

PERSONAL PRAYER As we close today, let's continue to exercise our prayer muscles. Write down some specific things you're thankful to the Lord for and pray back a prayer of thanksgiving.

You've covered a lot on prayer this session. Very well done! Bible study and prayer are two of the most foundational disciplines we can practice, which is why I devoted extra days to each. Throughout history, God's people have been people of prayer. They've lifted prayers of praise, thanksgiving, intercession, lament, petition, and forgiveness in full assurance that God heard and would answer. We must do the same.

They have also participated in another discipline that is closely tied to prayer. But I'm getting ahead of myself. We'll look at that one tomorrow. In the meantime, be a person of prayer. As the late Andrew Murray once said, prayer is ". . . the highest exercise of your privilege as a branch of the Vine."[27]

For a list of prayers in Scripture to aid you in your prayer time, see pages 74–75.

The Blessing of Confession

What I cover up I'm left with—what I open up receives not only the revealing of God, but also the healing of God.[28]

REUBEN WELCH

Confession is one of those disciplines we practice both privately with God and communally with others. We'll look at the gift of communal confession in Session Seven, which is different from confessing our sins and wayward attitudes to the Lord in our private times of prayer. Today we'll start by looking at the untrustworthiness of our hearts, but we'll end in a beloved psalm of repentance and restoration. For the sinners who fear their sins are beyond the cleansing power of God's forgiveness, He cleanses our inner beings white as snow. For the ones who feel fundamentally flawed, God literally creates new hearts! And if your fire for the Lord has died down to an ember, He reignites the joy of our salvation. We'll discover that confession is the entry point to such renewal.

> **PERSONAL REFLECTION** Is confession a regular part of your prayer life? Why or why not? Give this some thought.

Read Psalm 139:23-24.

True/False: We need God to search our hearts because we don't know ourselves as well as He knows us.

> **PERSONAL TAKE** How does this prayer from Psalm 139 relieve you of the pressure of having to search your own heart?

I love Psalm 139:23-24 because it's a catchall for the sins I'm aware of and the ones I don't even know are present. It's also the ultimate diagnostic prayer—*Lord, if I'm not where you want me to be, get me there. If something is offensive in me, lead me in the direction that matters eternally instead of one that is fleeting.* This psalm is a good one to pray, especially when we aren't sure where we've fallen short or where we've overdone it. It's also a good reminder that we can't trust our own hearts to lead us.

Read Jeremiah 17:9-10.

Why can't we trust our heart as our ultimate guide and standard?

Who is the only One worthy to examine our minds and hearts?

Read verse 14.

So we don't get too discouraged, what hope did Jeremiah offer in response to this news?

If we don't measure our actions against the truths of Scripture, our hearts will be the judge of us. And if the heart, prone to deceive us, is our judge, we'll justify gossip and greed, explain away lust, and celebrate what we should be running from. But when Jesus is the Examiner of our minds and Tester of our hearts, we can see our sins clearly, confess them, and receive His immeasurable forgiveness.

Still, what about those times when the knowledge of our sin and guilt seem unbearable before the Lord? King David knew this crushing grief well, leaving us a beloved record of his path of restoration. Psalm 51 is a famous prayer most scholars attribute to David, written after he was confronted about his adultery with Bathsheba. We learn a lot about confession from this prayer and a lot about God's merciful compassion and forgiveness.

Read Psalm 51 and examine verses 1-5. Was David trying to justify his sin and cover up what he'd done, or was he owning his actions? Take a moment to summarize his disposition before the Lord.

What two things did David ask for in verse 7?

Hyssop is a woody plant that was used in early-Israelite cleansing rituals.[29] It appears in Numbers 19:6,18 as part of the purification process for the people's sin. A hyssop branch was also used to smear the blood over the doorframes during Passover.[30] David, being well-aware of these practices, used the hyssop imagery to symbolize the cleansing of sin. He also used the imagery of snow. Nothing gleams purer or brighter than freshly fallen snow reflecting the light of the sun.

In Psalm 51:10, David asked God to _____ a clean heart in him.

The Hebrew word for create is *bārā'*, and it's an interesting choice for David to use.[31] Only God is the subject of this verb in the Old Testament, and it's the word used in Genesis to describe God creating the world out of nothing.[32] It's possible that David was asking God to do a miracle in him, to create a brand new heart within him. At the very least, David was aware that only God can cleanse and restore him.

PERSONAL REFLECTION Have you ever messed up so badly, sinned so deeply, that you knew God was the only One who could set things right inside you? Describe God's response toward you in that situation.

What did David ask God not to do in verse 11?

PERSONAL TAKE Out of all the things David feared could happen, why was being banished from God's presence or having the Holy Spirit removed from his life the worst thing he could imagine? Give this some thought.

I can't overstate how grateful I am that as believers we are safely and solidly in the Lord's hands (John 10:28-30) and that no sin can separate us from His love (Rom. 8:38-39). At the same time, our sin disrupts our fellowship with Christ. We must resist the tendency to think that just because our sin won't cost us our salvation that it doesn't cost us what we should most value—our intimacy with Jesus. Notice that David didn't ask to be spared from suffering, a loss, or even death. In his mind, the worst possible consequence of his sin was separation from God's presence. While we don't have to fear losing the Holy Spirit within us, we should be gutted over any sin that might break our fellowship with Him.

> **PERSONAL TAKE** Look back at Psalm 51:16-17. Why do you think brokenness and humility (genuine repentance) was more precious to God than David bringing Him the sacrificial offering of an animal?

Read Hebrews 10:10,18-23.

What offering has been made once and for all (v. 10)?

Fill in the blank. Because of Jesus' forgiveness of our sin, once and for all, there is no longer an _____ for sin (v. 18).

What did the author of Hebrews tell us to do in verse 22?

Psalm 51 ends with David asking God to restore Jerusalem so whole burnt offerings would be acceptable once again. But this time they would be righteous sacrifices, ones born out of a repentant and pure heart. Once Jesus replaced the old covenant with the new covenant of His blood, there was no longer a need for animal sacrifice because Jesus became the only and final sacrifice for us. Still, God delights in the person who is humble and contrite before Him. He loves for us to draw near to Him in full assurance—to regularly confess our sins so our daily communion with Christ flows without inhibition.

> **PERSONAL PRAYER** Return to Psalm 139 and pray verses 23-24. Listen closely to what God reveals and spend time in confession. May you receive the refreshment of Christ's forgiveness.

You've accomplished so much in these first two weeks. Excellent work! I'm already looking forward to Session Four where we'll study some of the more expressive spiritual disciplines. If these first two weeks have felt somewhat introspective, prepare thyself to emote. In the meantime, put into practice something new you've learned about Bible study and prayer. Before you know it, these disciplines will become habits.

Pray

Prayer can be hard work. But it is also a joyful and rewarding practice. As we continue to deepen our life of prayer, we'll find that we crave it when the busyness of life has edged it out.

FOR AN EFFECTIVE PRAYER LIFE, HERE ARE SOME HELPFUL TIPS:

1. **Designate a consistent time and place.** Obviously, there are exceptions. Some of us travel and can't always be in the same place at the same time every day. But consistency will help aid in the routine.

2. **Use a journal.** Sometimes I like to write my prayers out in my journal. Other times I simply make a list of the people and situations I'm praying over and I'll include those in my journal as well. Journaling provides a wonderful record of what God has done in my life and what has been important to me over the years.

IDEAS TO HELP YOU IN PRAYER:

1. **Pray Scripture.** What better words to say to God than the ones He's given us.

Pray prayers from the Bible. There are lots of beautiful, powerful prayers in Scripture. Here are a few of my favorites:

OLD TESTAMENT	NEW TESTAMENT
1 Samuel 2:1-10	Matthew 6:9-13
2 Chronicles 6:14-42	Ephesians 1:15-19
Nehemiah 1:5-11	Ephesians 3:14-21
Nehemiah 9:5-37	Philippians 1:3-11
Daniel 9:4-19	Colossians 1:9-14
Habakkuk 3:1-19	
Any of the Psalms	

Pray Scripture passages. Perhaps a verse, series of verses, or even a chapter that has meant a lot to you. It may be filled with words of praise, petition, or even instruction you want the Lord to help you follow. Personalize that passage and pray it to the Lord. Turning passages into prayers can also be effective in helping you know what to pray. There are some examples of verses to pray on the following page.

OLD TESTAMENT	NEW TESTAMENT
Joshua 24:15	Matthew 11:28-30
Proverbs 3:5-7	John 14:27
Isaiah 40:28-31	John 15:5-8
Isaiah 43:1-3a	Ephesians 6:10-19
Lamentations 3:25-27	Colossians 1:15-20

Again, this is just a brief sampling of the many places you could turn in the Old and New Testaments for passages to pray and make your own.

2. **Follow a formula.** Pray using a simple method that helps remind you what to pray and keeps you on track.

ACTS	Adoration / Confession / Thanksgiving / Supplication
PRAY	Pray / Repent / Ask / Yield to Christ
THREE Rs	Rejoice / Repent / Request[33]

3. **Organize your prayers.** Set up a system where you emphasize different prayer requests on different days. For example:

SUNDAY	Family or close relationships
MONDAY	People you want to reach out to
TUESDAY	Intercession for those sick or in need
WEDNESDAY	Those who don't know Christ
THURSDAY	Your church community
FRIDAY	The persecuted church
SATURDAY	Mission and ministry opportunities

4. **Pray with others.** This is a big one! I can often pray longer and with more focus when I'm praying with others. I'm amazed at how praying with other people bonds you with them, which is why it's difficult to hold grudges with those you regularly pray with! Praying with others holds me accountable. And while it can be a vulnerable and uncomfortable practice at first, I encourage you to take that step! The blessings of group prayer and the bonds of friendship that can come out of it are unrivaled. Just a reminder: praying with others shouldn't take the place of your personal times of prayer, but it will be a wonderful addition.

5. **Pray continually.** Remember, talking to God doesn't require a reservation. He lives IN you. Carry on a constant conversation.

WATCH SESSION THREE VIDEO

DISCUSSION QUESTIONS

What's something that really stood out to you in the video teaching?

Would you say you're better at studying God's Word or praying?
Explain.

How would you define the current state of your prayer life? What seems
to be the biggest hindrance for you when it comes to praying?

How does our view of God affect our prayer life?

Have you ever found yourself in the spot where prayer seems to be just
a religious activity, such as the religious leaders who stood on the street
corners to be seen? Why do you think that happens? What's the danger
in this?

Why is it so important that we understand we pray to a personal God?

How is it comforting and encouraging to know we pray to a God who
already knows what we need?

What does it mean that prayer is not transactional but relational? Why
do we sometimes struggle with this?

Jesus taught that our heavenly Father is eager to give us good gifts.
How has God proven Himself to be a good, trustworthy, and responsive
Father to you in your prayer life?

Video sessions available for purchase or rent
at lifeway.com/encounteringgod

SESSION FOUR

Express

JOURNALING THE SESSION

Use this page throughout your session of study. We've given you some prompts, but feel free to write other thoughts and questions to help you learn and process the spiritual disciplines of worship, fasting, thanksgiving, and celebration.

PREPARING FOR THE SESSION

Before you start your work this session, journal some of your thoughts about the disciplines of worship, fasting, thanksgiving, and celebration. How have you practiced these disciplines in the past? What has hindered your practice of these disciplines? What do you hope to get out of this session?

DURING THE SESSION

What are some key things you're learning this session about the disciplines of worship, fasting, thanksgiving, and celebration?

REVIEWING THE SESSION

What are your biggest takeaways from this session, and how will you put them into practice?

Session Four Introduction

Worship reminds us of who God is and who we are in relation to Him. Worshiping the one true God is perhaps the most grounding practice of human existence. To set our gaze upon Creator God, to bow down before King Jesus, to adore the Holy Spirit is to exalt the One who is infinitely greater than us as humans and grander than all creation. Simply put, worship properly positions us.

You may have heard it said that if we don't worship God, we'll worship something. I suspect this is true. We only need to look around at humanity's tendency to cast ourselves on the altar of beauty, money, pleasure, powerful people, and important experiences. I get caught up in this, too. I remember talking with my youth pastor on a particular afternoon not long after entering high school. He asked me what I found most challenging about this new season in life. I remember my response being something along the lines of, "I care too much about what the cool kids think." I wouldn't have used the language of worship at the time, but essentially that's what it was. I worshiped the popular people, or worshiped popularity itself.

This tug on my heart hasn't completely ceased, but it's diminished greatly over the years. The heartache of worshiping anything other than Jesus has left its share of good-reminder scars. On a more positive note, worshiping the one true God has been restorative to my soul. One of the most freeing aspects of worship is that it reminds us God is in control. Worship rightly orders our desires and agendas. It keeps our wins and losses in check—none of our circumstances get too big, good or bad, because everything is proportionately measured in light of His majesty, love, and care for us.

I used to wonder why in the world God was jealous for our worship (Ex. 20:5). Is He so egotistical that He created millions of people to praise Him? Is His self-esteem so low He demands we acknowledge Him? Is He threatened by all the false gods out there that might steal our worship of Him? This really did perplex and bother me in my earlier years, yet Scripture answers these questions. In its pages we discover that the ability to worship God is one of His gifts to us. He does not need us to worship Him; rather, He delights in our worship because He knows we need to worship!

Worship is a difficult spiritual discipline to define because it takes on so many forms. We sing in our corporate worship services and by ourselves in our kitchens and cars to our worship playlists. We may lift our hands in adoration or humbly bow in confession as we encounter His holiness. Worship can also look like service. We worship with our lips but also with our time, resources, and money as we give to the Lord's work. Worship will sometimes pour forth as lament and other times as a full-on celebration. Because worship is our response to who God is and what He has done, it only makes sense we've been given a worship palette of countless colors with which to express ourselves to Him.

I don't know about you, but in our selfie-obsessed world, in our social media frenzy where everyone is longing to be seen, I find myself yearning to focus on someone other than me—to individually and collectively acknowledge God's holiness and other-than-ness, to esteem Christ, the only One worthy of our praise, and to humble myself before Him who is infinitely grand yet endearingly near.

> One of the most freeing aspects of worship is that it reminds us God is in control.

Worship Through Adoration

Worship is our response to the overtures of love from the heart of the Father.[1]

RICHARD FOSTER

As stated in this session's introduction, worship reminds us who God is and who we are in relation to Him. I need this reorientation often. I recently attended my church's monthly staff meeting, which is saying something because I'm not on staff. But when I heard my friends Leo and Monica were leading worship at the meeting, I invited myself and found a spot on the front row. (This is exactly the only meeting in the history of my existence that I have chosen to attend without it being mandatory.) I went because I needed to worship the living God, to sing His praise alongside my brothers and sisters in Christ, and to surrender to His leading. I was especially desperate to worship because of a pressing situation I have no answers for. I needed to tell the Lord, and remind myself in the process, that He is good, that He is all-powerful, that He is able, that He shines light into the darkness! Oh yes, I needed to worship.

Worship is our response to the holiness, goodness, and grandeur of God. As we noted in the introduction, worship takes on many forms, several of which we'll look at this session. Today we'll study one that affects our physical posture. In the Old Testament, the Hebrew word used to describe this form of worship is *shāchāh*. It means to *bow (self) down, to prostrate oneself, to crouch, to fall down, to humbly beseech, to do reverence, to worship.*[2] This type of worship could be described as a physical expression of what our heart is feeling and mind is thinking toward God.

Let's do a brief survey of Scripture to see how different people worshiped in this way in different circumstances.

Read each passage listed and answer the corresponding questions. Consider each context and what motivated each worshiper's response. (I provided some context when necessary.)

EXODUS 4:27-31

Why did the people worship?

EXODUS 34:1-9

Why did Moses worship?

NEHEMIAH 8:1-3,6

This event took place sometime after the Israelite remnant returned to Jerusalem. The people gathered together, bringing back former practices.

What did Ezra read to the people that prompted their worship? How did they respond?

PSALM 95:3-7

Why did the psalmist encourage this type of worship?

Let's look at a passage out of 2 Chronicles. Much of 1 and 2 Chronicles is dedicated to the building and description of Solomon's temple and how the people of God worshiped in those days. While 1 and 2 Chronicles include much of the same material that's in 1 and 2 Samuel and 1 and 2 Kings, the author's emphasis is on worship. This is a helpful fact when reading through these two historical books.

Read 2 Chronicles 7:1-3.

> PERSONAL REFLECTION Have you ever been so overwhelmed by the presence of God that you fell or knelt down before Him? That would be to *shāchāh* the Lord (the Hebrew word used in the passages you just read).[3] Describe the situation, what you felt, and why you responded the way you did. Your response might be a good one to share with your group.

I haven't personally experienced quite what was described in 2 Chronicles 7, but I can remember a few precious times when I was so aware of the presence of the Lord I went straight to my knees or even facedown.

One that comes to mind happened in the Amazon during JMI's Jungle Pastors' Conference. I had just finished teaching out of John 15 about abiding in Christ. As I closed my Bible, one of the women started singing in response. A trickle of voices joined her. By the chorus, everyone was singing. Louder and louder they worshiped and cried out. I had this sense that our holy rumble could raise the tin roof from its wooden joists. You could actually feel the worship. I knew little of what was being sung because it was all in Portuguese, but the object of their words was unmistakable. My only reasonable response was to get down on the ground before Almighty God. In the middle of the Amazon jungle, the Lord Himself had come to meet with us.

> Before we move to the New Testament, let's briefly survey a few other expressions of worship found in Psalms. Next to each reference, list the worshipful expressions found in each passage.
>
> PSALM 47:1-2
>
> PSALM 95:1-2
>
> PSALM 96:1-3
>
> PSALM 149:1-3

PERSONAL TAKE After surveying physical postures of worship in the Old Testament, why do you think it's important to express ourselves in worship? This will look different for everyone.

The parallel term to *shāchāh* in the New Testament is the word *proskuneo*. It means "to incline the face to the ground: to prostrate oneself before someone as an act of reverence, fear, or supplication . . ."[4] We'll now look at how this type of worship is directed specifically to Jesus.

Read the following passages and briefly describe each worship scene.

MATTHEW 2:1-2,9-11

What caused the wise men to worship?

MATTHEW 14:27-33

What did Jesus do that caused the disciples to worship? Why do you think they responded with this form of worship?

MATTHEW 28:5-10

Describe why falling before Jesus was the only reasonable response in this situation.

JOHN 9:1-7,35-38

What caused the formerly blind man to worship Jesus?

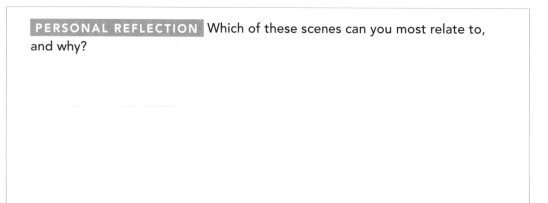

PERSONAL REFLECTION Which of these scenes can you most relate to, and why?

When I'm in Brazil, many of my Amazonian friends dance, shout, and lie on the ground when they worship. I love it because they inspire me by their expressive, passionate love for Jesus. Noting the many references to *proskuneo* and *shāchāh* and looking at other worshipful expressions shows the importance of physically expressing ourselves in worship. This is not to the exclusion of stillness or silence, which also can be a way of esteeming the Lord. No judgment here. It's just that we tend to hold back on the more demonstrative ways of worshiping often found in Scripture, and I think it's important to ask *why*.

When I'm in my car listening to my favorite songs, I sing out loud. When I'm cheering at a game, I yell! If I haven't seen you in a while, I want to hug you. If I were ever to meet someone like the Queen of England, my inclination would be to bow. Our bodies are designed to outwardly express our inward passions. And maybe that last phrase—*inward passions*—is the key. Perhaps we're not as passionate about Jesus as we want to be and therefore our outward expression of worship is lacking.

Sometimes when I'm lacking in my love for the Lord, I personalize Ephesians 3:17-19.

Dear Father, root me and establish me in love so that I can comprehend with all the saints what is the length and width, height and depth of Your love. And help me know Christ's love that surpasses knowledge so that I may be filled with all the fullness of God.

PERSONAL PRAYER Pray Ephesians 3:17-19 for yourself. I believe the more we grasp God's infinite love for us, the more we'll want to express our praise to Him.

PERSONAL PRACTICE Take a moment to get into a physical posture of worship before the Lord. Spend time praying, praising, or simply being still before Him.

Beautiful job today my friends. What a privilege we have to express ourselves in worship. I'm already excited about tomorrow when we'll look at another outward form of worship. Whatever you do, don't get overwhelmed. Remember, we're not called to be experts at the spiritual disciplines. We're simply called to be apprentices of Jesus. Let's keep following Him.

We're not called to be experts at the spiritual disciplines. We're simply called to be apprentices of Jesus.

Worshiping Through Our Actions

The life of true holiness is rooted in the soil of awed adoration.[5]

J. I. PACKER

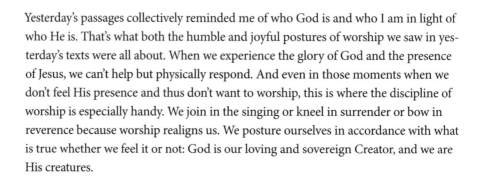

Yesterday's passages collectively reminded me of who God is and who I am in light of who He is. That's what both the humble and joyful postures of worship we saw in yesterday's texts were all about. When we experience the glory of God and the presence of Jesus, we can't help but physically respond. And even in those moments when we don't feel His presence and thus don't want to worship, this is where the discipline of worship is especially handy. We join in the singing or kneel in surrender or bow in reverence because worship realigns us. We posture ourselves in accordance with what is true whether we feel it or not: God is our loving and sovereign Creator, and we are His creatures.

My sister Katie used to babysit for a three-year-old who tried to talk her into all kinds of things by saying, "We are the bosses of ourselves!" It's one of our favorite quotes to this day. And while I used to think living according to this line of thinking would be a dream, as I've aged, nothing could be more fearful a thought. Worship reminds me precisely that I am not the boss of myself—that the world isn't all about me. Worship reestablishes my understanding that God is holy and beautiful and powerful and glorious and that I submit to Him. This is especially wonderful because He is good and He loves us.

If yesterday's study was about worshiping God through physical expression, today is about worshiping Him through our actions. Differentiating between the two in Scripture can be challenging because oftentimes the word *worship* is used to describe both. We'll try to clarify this today as we see how God's people worshiped with their lives. And how we can, too.

> **QUICK REVIEW** Yesterday we looked at the Hebrew word *shāchāh* and the Greek word *proskuneo*. What basic meaning do they both share?

Read Exodus 3:1-12.

Near the end of Genesis, a famine prompted the patriarch Jacob, his sons, and their families to leave the land of Canaan and move to Egypt. By God's providence, Jacob's son, Joseph, had already been living in Egypt for many years and was second in command under Pharaoh, so he was able to provide food and land for his brothers and their families. Jacob's extended family continued to grow over many generations into what would eventually become the nation of Israel. However, as they grew, so did Egypt's oppressive rule. The people of God were no longer free to do what God had created them to do.

> Who did God send to deliver Israel from Egypt?

> According to verse 12, what were the Israelites to do once they were out of Egypt?

The Hebrew word for *worship* in Exodus 3:12 is 'ā*bad,* and it means *to work* or *to serve.*[6] Your Bible translation may even use the word *serve* instead of *worship* here. The word also carries the idea of working for the Lord in the context of a religious service in the spirit of joyful liberation.[7] Simply put, 'ā*bad* is the kind of worship that is service and ministry-oriented.

The phrase "Let my people go, so they may worship me" is a theme of Exodus, found in 7:16; 8:20; 9:1; 9:13; 10:26.

> How does worship through serving and doing differ from the kind of worship we studied yesterday?

PERSONAL TAKE When you think of all the purposes for which God could have delivered the Israelites from the bondage of Egypt, why do you think this kind of worship was the central reason? Keep in mind the idea of 'ā*bad* when answering.

Throughout the Old Testament, we find that one of the ways the people worshiped God was through active participation. They did certain things that brought Him delight. Much of this worship consisted in walking out the Law of Moses, keeping the feasts, going to the temple, offering sacrifices and tithes, and not turning away from Him to false gods. Even at the time of Christ's birth, we see a special woman serving this way in the temple.

Read Luke 2:36-38.

> What did Anna do night and day? (The expression "serving God night and day" doesn't mean she literally lived at the temple twenty-four hours a day; it was used to show her devotion.)

Anna chose a lifetime of service to God over remarriage.[8] This is certainly not a prescription for anyone, but Anna's decision reflects how deeply she valued the privilege of serving the Lord.

> **PERSONAL REFLECTION** Have you or your family willingly given something up so you could actively worship the Lord in some way? This might mean working less hours to pour into your family, sacrificing sleep to disciple someone, forgoing a vacation to go on a mission trip, letting go of a hobby to play in a worship band . . .

The concept of worshiping God through active ministry not only didn't disappear at Christ's coming, it expanded in the New Testament. The Greek counterpart to the Hebrew word *'ābad* is *latreuō* and it, too, means *to serve* or *minister*. (It's the word used in relationship to Anna in Luke 2:37.)[9]

Read Hebrews 9:11-14.

> According to verse 12, what did Jesus do for us once and for all?

> According to verse 14, what is the purpose of having our consciences cleansed by Jesus?

We have been set free from guilt, shame, sin, and condemnation for the gift of being able to worship God by serving Him (*latreuō*). Just as God rescued the Israelites from the bondage of Egypt to free them to serve Him in tents, tabernacles, and the temple, Jesus rescued us so that we are free to serve Him in every area of our lives. I love this truth because it means our lives matter. Hear this personally: You have a purpose. Your life is meant to count for His glory.

Read Romans 12:1.

> What did Paul say is our reasonable act of worship or service (*latreuō*)?

> Your life is meant to count for His glory.

The late scholar William Hendriksen said, "Paul is thinking about the *action* of worshiping, the wholehearted consecration of heart, mind, will, words, and deeds, in fact of all one is, has, and does, to God. Nothing less!" (emphasis mine).[10] My hope is that this doesn't overwhelm you but excites you. God wants all of you. He loves you that much and knows that worshiping Him with your whole life provides the most fulfillment you can have.

PERSONAL REFLECTION How does Romans 12:1 broaden your view of what worship is supposed to look like in your life? Where does it challenge you?

You've covered a lot of ground these past two days, and you've done great! I know the Greek and Hebrew words can sometimes get tedious, but in this case their meanings really help us see worship as both physical adoration and a life of active service. We'll close today with a final personal reflection.

PERSONAL REFLECTION As you consider worship through service and worship through adoration, which comes most naturally to you, and why?

What can you do to bring the form of worship that currently comes less naturally to you into a regular rhythm of your life?

Feasting by Fasting

In fasting, we learn how to suffer happily as we feast on God.[11]

DALLAS WILLARD

The spiritual discipline of fasting could have fit in several sessions of this study. It could have easily gone next to prayer, confession, or even simplicity. As we'll continue to discover, the spiritual disciplines are as interconnected as vertebrae, each one working in concert with the others. I chose to place fasting alongside worship mostly because (drumroll) I ran out of space in last session's study on prayer. The other more-spiritual reason is that fasting is absolutely a form of worship. In fasting, we humble ourselves by abstaining from food to seek the face of God.

I realize that people can fast for weight loss or health benefits, but the fasting we find in Scripture is for the purpose of seeking God in a deeper way. Biblical fasting is also specifically about going without food and possibly drink for a set amount of time. We may say we're going to "fast" from television or social media or some form of entertainment we really enjoy, and while highly beneficial, this is abstaining, not fasting. Fasting always has to do with abstaining from food. *(See note at the end of this session.)

I'll admit I was hesitant to include this discipline for fear of scaring someone away. Please don't flee the premises clutching a cheeseburger, which was absolutely my gut reaction when first learning about what felt like the most treacherous of all the disciplines. I have often wondered, *Why on earth would anyone ever voluntarily skip a pancake?* I can't tell you how deeply I've searched the Scriptures for the spiritual discipline of eating—it's the one I've been training for all my life.

I learned about and practiced fasting at an early age. My earliest memory of this discipline is fasting with my youth group in junior high. I'm grateful for those earlier experiences because they exposed me to this lesser-practiced discipline at a young age. For me, fasting was part of the Christian landscape, even if the people who traveled to its territory were few and far between.

This still seems to be the case. Out of all the spiritual disciplines, fasting may be the one we practice the least. So the question is: *Why should we fast?* One simple reason is that Jesus and His disciples fasted. This alone should cause us to want to consider it. But beyond their example, today we'll learn some of the *why* behind fasting as well as the many benefits of it. We'll also see how Jesus changed the nature of fasting, transforming it into something we couldn't have seen coming.

Read Matthew 6:16.

Jesus said, "_____ you fast."

What does this tell us about what Jesus assumed His followers were doing?

Fasting was part of Israel's way of life throughout the Old Testament, and it was part of Jewish and Christian life in the New. Since today's single lesson on fasting can't begin to be exhaustive, we'll highlight several reasons in Scripture that people fasted, ending with the reason I think might be most central for us today.

Read 1 Samuel 7:1-6.

In a sentence or two, describe the situation in which this fast took place.

In this instance, what response(s) most closely accompanied the people's fasting? (Circle the correct answer(s).)

Pleaded for help   Confessed/repented   Prayed for others   Mourned

Read 2 Samuel 1:11-12.

In a sentence or two, describe the situation in which this fast took place.

In this instance, what response(s) most closely accompanied the people's fasting? (Circle the correct answer(s).)

Pleaded for help   Confessed/repented   Prayed for others   Mourned

Read 2 Samuel 12:15-23.

In a sentence or two, describe the situation in which this fast took place.

In this instance, what response(s) most closely accompanied the people's fasting? (Circle the correct answer(s).)

Pleaded for help   Confessed/repented   Prayed for others   Mourned

Read Nehemiah 1:1-4.

In a sentence or two, describe the situation in which this fast took place.

In this instance, what response(s) most closely accompanied the people's fasting? (Circle the correct answer(s).)

Pleaded for help   Confessed/repented   Prayed for others   Mourned

Read Esther 3:13; 4:1-3,15-17.

In a sentence or two, describe the situation in which this fast took place.

In this instance, what response(s) most closely accompanied the people's fasting? (Circle the correct answer(s).)

Pleaded for help   Confessed/repented   Prayed for others   Mourned

---

PERSONAL TAKE Surveying these passages gives us a sense of the environments in which fasting took place during ancient times. What common threads did you discover? Use the following prompt to help you answer: *People fasted when they were . . .*

A NEW COVENANT TRANSITION

My friend Kim helped me with this study by going through it before it went to print. In response to the previous question, she said, "People fasted when they were overwhelmed." I'm not sure there's a better way to put it. Whether overwhelmed by guilt, sadness, sickness, war, or sin, people have been driven to fast before God. Interestingly, fasting is mentioned much less often in the New Testament. In Acts 13:1-3, the apostles prayed and fasted as they set Barnabas and Saul apart for the work of the ministry. In Acts 14:21-23, they prayed and fasted before selecting elders. The prophetess Anna served God by prayer and fasting in the temple (Luke 2:37).

Most of the references in the New Testament just acknowledge that the people fasted rather than why they fasted. Jesus did, however, have something to say about how His followers were to fast.

Read Matthew 6:16-18.

> **PERSONAL TAKE** What about the hypocrites' disposition while fasting seems really different from the disposition of those we just read about in the Old Testament?

Turn a few pages forward to Matthew 9:14-15. Here Jesus referred to Himself as the groom at a wedding and His disciples as part of the wedding party, feasting.

What was the complaint of John the Baptist's disciples?

What reason did Jesus give for why His disciples weren't fasting at the time?

I know what you're thinking. Praise the Lord! Jesus Himself has spoken! We have a biblical case for why we need never fast and can eat burritos for the rest of our lives. Maybe. But probably not. What I think was happening here is not that fasting was going away; rather, the ways in which God's people fasted and the reasons for which they fasted were changing. It's true that because of Christ's coming we as the people of God have gone from fasting to feasting! But on occasion, we'll get to physically remind ourselves of this reality by fasting from food so we can feast on God Himself. Here's what I mean.

Read Matthew 4:1-4.

What did Jesus say nourishes us in addition to physical bread?

How does God's Word nourish you? Be specific. (Think in spiritual terms. But also think about the ways His Word fuels other areas of your life such as your work, emotions, relationships, parenting, sense of well-being, purpose, and more.)

Read John 4:31-34.

What kind of food did Jesus have to eat (vv. 32,34)?

Read John 6:22-35.

Why were the people intently looking for Jesus (v. 26)?

What did Jesus tell the people to do and not do in verse 27, and why?

What did Jesus call Himself in verse 35?

I love what Dallas Willard said about fasting: "Fasting confirms our utter dependence upon God by finding in him a source of sustenance beyond food."[12]

How does Jesus as the Bread of life encourage you to set aside a meal or two or three for the purpose of feasting on His presence?

I don't believe the reasons for fasting under the old covenant are obsolete under the new, but I do believe Jesus changes our experience of fasting. I believe we can and should fast for guidance, healing, direction, on behalf of others (intercession), in pursuit of spiritual breakthroughs, and more. But I believe one of the greatest reasons we can fast is simply in pursuit of a deeper experience of Christ. In closing, I would love to share with you some of the benefits I've received and lessons I've learned from fasting over the years.

1. **Fasting is not a way to manipulate God to do what you want Him to do (Isa. 58).** When we fast, we're voluntarily putting ourselves in a place of weakness and dependence upon God, trusting Him with the results of our fast.

2. **When we fast, we're forgoing something natural in pursuit of the supernatural.** Jesus feasted on bread that was not of this world. Fasting has helped me become more aware of the spiritual realm that is often obscured by my earthly yearnings.

3. **When we fast, we're practicing the needed discipline of saying no to ourselves and yes to God.** In a culture that prizes the ideas of *on-demand*, *you deserve it*, and *don't go without*, we desperately need to tell ourselves no on occasion. While this may seem inhibiting at first, it's paradoxically liberating. When I have control over my body, when I'm not "hangry" several times a week, when my temperament isn't ruled by my next meal, there is freedom.

4. **Fasting is a great way of taking the focus off myself and placing it on God and others.** Our Justice & Mercy International staff fasts sunset to sunset once a month. When all I want is a piece of pizza, there's something good and powerful about interceding for those in the Amazon who may not have eaten for days or for our vulnerable children in Moldova who often live in abusive homes. Fasting puts life in perspective and aligns our hearts with the Lord's.

5. **Fasting teaches me contentment.** When my body isn't immediately satisfied or life deals me a series of disappointments, fasting helps me practice the habit of going to the Lord and seeking satisfaction from Him instead of what is readily available to me (like my prized stash of dark chocolate peanut butter cups that solve a multitude of ailments).

I'm sure there are more reasons, but here's the bottom line: fasting is worth it, my dear friends. I pray you will incorporate it into your semi-regular rhythm of life. Plan to fast with some friends. Start small if you've never fasted before, maybe by skipping one or two meals only. Drink plenty of water and don't overexert yourself. Gather with others to pray during your fasting. Plan times to be with the Lord or with others in fellowship. And most of all, feast.

Important note about fasting: If you have any health issues, consult your doctor about whether fasting is safe for you. Also, if you have a history of eating disorders or if fasting is a negative trigger for you, I would encourage you to abstain from something other than food that you really enjoy (social media, television, a certain drink, or an activity.) In summary, if you can healthily fast from food, I encourage you to practice this discipline. But if fasting is not healthy for you physically, emotionally, or psychologically, simply abstain for a time from something you enjoy for the sake of feasting on the Bread of life.

Cultivating a Thankful Heart

It's one thing to be grateful. It's another to give thanks. Gratitude is what you feel. Thanksgiving is what you do.[13]

TIM KELLER

Today, I want you to begin our study.

> **PERSONAL REFLECTION** What are you most thankful to the Lord for today? Don't skip this. I know it's crossing your mind. Take a moment to practice thankfulness.

I suppose I should just come out with it and confess that cultivating a discipline of thanksgiving is one of my weaker points. I tend to see what's wrong, what needs attention, what could be ever so slightly improved upon before I see what is good and right. Thanking the Lord for His many answered prayers and unexpected gifts readily falls by the wayside of busyness and pressing matters. Yet it is in all manner of life's soil that I should sow seeds of thankfulness. Each prayer of gratitude blossoms into a fragrant reminder that God's past goodness will surely prove faithful in my present hour of need.

Today we'll spend the whole of our study in Psalm 107. We'll take it in sections, thoughtfully pondering the goodness of the Lord, casting seeds of thanks along the way.

Psalm 107 was written after the Jews returned to Jerusalem from their seventy-year exile in Babylon. We find the regathered people of God singing this communal song of praise for God's redemption. What a remarkable setting!

Read Psalm 107:1-3.

Why did the psalmist say we are to give thanks (v. 1)?

What types of people are to proclaim that God has redeemed them (v. 2)?

From what and where were the people gathered (vv. 2-3)?

The concept of redemption expresses the idea of regaining something that was once lost.[14] When we speak of being "redeemed," our mind probably goes to the New Testament meaning of the word and how we have personally experienced redemption through Christ. We absolutely should be thankful for that redemption. But the use of the word here is broader than that. It's more along the lines of how God has moved to help His people in dire circumstances, how His redemption and deliverance are seen in all areas of our lives.

PERSONAL THANKS In a few sentences, how has God redeemed you from a difficult situation?

Starting at verse four, the psalm is broken up into four sections that describe God's deliverance from difficult circumstances. We may not find ourselves near death, facing wild seas, or as homeless nomads or prisoners, but we've probably all faced impossible circumstances that only God could deliver us from. Part of me wanted to reflect on a "lighter" psalm of thanksgiving, one where we find God's people thanking Him for delicious wine, savory olives, a booming harvest of grain, numerous cattle, and so forth. I'm here for all of that. But our richest thanks often spring from being delivered out of our most hopeless circumstances. This is Psalm 107.

A HOME FOR THE HOMELESS
Read verses 4-9.

Briefly describe the trying circumstance the people faced.

What did God do for them?

What were they to thank Him for (vv. 8-9)?

In addition to this section being reminiscent of the Jews returning from Babylon to Jerusalem, it also brings to mind the wilderness wanderings the Israelites endured for forty years after their release from Egypt. These verses meant a lot to me when I was trying to find my footing in Nashville two decades ago. I desperately longed for community, to be established, and to find a peaceful place to live. After a few tumultuous years, God settled me in a house, surrounded me with friends who love the Lord, and established my work. I never read these verses without remembering the pain and wandering of that time. I also never read them without a heart of thanks for the ways He's so peacefully and securely settled me.

> **PERSONAL REFLECTION** Verse 8 tells us once again to give thanks. In what specific ways has the Lord settled you and filled you with good things? (Even if some areas still feel unsettled, focus on where He has given you a firm foundation in Him.)

FREEDOM FOR THE CAPTIVE
Read verses 10-16.

Briefly describe the trying circumstance of the people.

What did God do for them?

What were they to thank Him for (vv. 15-16)?

We often have this impression that God is happy and eager to rescue all the godly people, the church-goers, the Bible study-filler-outters. But the undeserving? The disobedient? Well, they're a different matter. But look again at verse 11.

Who did God come for?

And what did He do for them (vv. 13-16)?

God valiantly comes for the rebellious and those who hated His instruction. The weight of His judgment eventually compelled them to cry to Him for help. He tore the chains apart that held them and rescued them from darkness. Can anyone see a glimmer of Jesus here?

> PERSONAL THANKS Pause. Thank God for a time He rescued you when you least deserved it.

HEALING FOR THE SUFFERER
Read verses 17-22.

Briefly describe the trying circumstance of the people.

What did God do for them?

How were they to thank Him (vv. 21-22)?

You may have remembered verse 20 from Day Five of Session Two: "He sent his word and healed them." God's Word is an agent of healing. It literally heals us from the inside out; it rescues from darkness, delivers from the pit, and breaks the chains that hold us.

> PERSONAL REFLECTION What's one way that God's Word has healed you or brought change in a difficult situation?

PEACE FOR THE OVERWHELMED
Read verses 23-32.

Briefly describe the trying circumstance of the people.

What was their skill able to accomplish according to verse 27?

What did God do for them?

In addition to giving thanks, what else were the redeemed encouraged to do (v. 32)?

There is a certain helplessness to being at sea in a storm-tossed boat at the merciless discretion of crashing waves. The poor sea merchants in this passage hadn't done anything to deserve the tempest in their midst, unlike those in the previous section of the psalm. (Not all trials or hardship are a result of sin—I hope that's an encouragement to you.) To make matters worse in such a terrifying time, the sailors' nautical experience was useless (v. 27). I wonder if you've ever faced an overwhelming situation when your skills and resources were futile? I certainly have. It's in those times when God supernaturally stills a storm and leads us to a safe harbor that we begin to know Him as our Great Redeemer.

The final section of Psalm 107:33-43 breaks from the earlier pattern, yet it's a continued testimony of what God was doing for His people since the exile. He had not left them in a desert wasteland; He'd settled and established them. They were growing fruitful harvests. They were multiplying. God was continuing to bless them.

Read verses 33-43.

PERSONAL TAKE Why do you think the psalmist said the wise person will pay attention to God's past works and reflect on His loving acts (v. 43)? In other words, why is thankful remembrance a practice of the wise?

PERSONAL REFLECTION How does remembering God's past deeds and specific work in your life cultivate a heart of thankfulness?

The repetition of, "Let them give thanks to the LORD for his faithful love and his wondrous works for all humanity" is a reminder in and of itself that regularly pausing to be thankful is an important practice throughout our day. Perhaps more than anything, practicing thanksgiving grows us into thankful people. So I hope today has reminded you of the faithful works of the Lord—the ones He's worked for Israel and the ones He's brought about for you. "The upright see it and rejoice" (v. 42).

Practicing for the Party That Awaits

Celebration gives us the strength to live in all the other Disciplines.[15]

RICHARD FOSTER

Celebration is primarily a communal activity. I suppose you can celebrate alone, but who will bear witness to what is being celebrated? Who will hold forth the glasses at your toast? More importantly, who will help you do the dishes?

This is purely anecdotal, but it seems to me that we modern-day Christians know how to celebrate. We aren't at a loss for wedding receptions, birthday parties, retirement bashes, and gender reveal cupcake gatherings. We can make a party out of just about anything. Where things get a little scant on our calendar are the engagements that revolve around celebrating who Christ is and what He's done. Yes, we have Christmas and Easter. But we have to admit that even these holidays have been run over by Santa and the Easter Bunny and all manner of shopping and cooking and reruns of *Elf*. Stay with me. I promise not to ruin today's study on celebration with all my cynicism.

What I'm trying to get at is this: We may be professional celebrators, but that doesn't mean we're especially good at celebrating the things the Israelites or the early church celebrated. As one of my favorite authors and Bible teachers Reuben Welch once said, "Early Christians . . . often met together to express their oneness in Christ—around the teaching, around the Word, around the sacraments, and around prayer. *They were being together as Christians, not just Christians being together*" (emphasis mine).[16] He gets me with that last line every time. I want to be better at having more purposeful celebrations around what binds us together as believers.

Feasting and celebration were a significant part of the lives of the ancient Israelites. They gathered together three times a year to celebrate the goodness of God. These holiday festivals provided strength and cohesion to the people of Israel. They knew how to throw a party. Today we'll look at the seasonal celebrations of God's goodness that were part of the fabric of ancient Israelite life.

Look up 2 Chronicles 8:12-13.

> What three festivals are mentioned?
> 1.
>
> 2.
>
> 3.

The Feast of Unleavened Bread is better known to us as Passover. God commanded the Israelites to celebrate Passover to commemorate the night they placed the blood of a lamb over their door-posts in Egypt so the angel of judgment would pass over their homes. The next day God began to deliver Israel out of the bondage of Egypt.

Read Deuteronomy 16:1-3.

> Why were they to continue to celebrate the Passover year after year (v. 3)?

The Festival of Weeks was a celebration of the day the Israelites gathered at the base of Mount Sinai when the Lord appeared to Moses on behalf of the people. It was exactly fifty days after the first Passover took place in Egypt. Interestingly, during the time between the Old and New Testaments, Jews viewed this festival as marking the time when the law was given.[17]

Read Exodus 19:3-6.

> What kind of people did God declare that Israel would be (vv. 5-6)?

Read Deuteronomy 16:9-12.

> How were they to celebrate this special feast, and why?

The Festival of Booths (or Tabernacles or Shelters) is a personal favorite of mine because it's reminiscent of a weeklong camping extravaganza where all the Israelites and their families set up shelters and lived in them for a week. They did this to commemorate the ways the Lord took care of them through their wilderness wanderings. I'm not a huge camper, but I could get behind the idea of a whole bunch of us getting out of our normal environments in maybe, say, a glamping situation, and recounting God's faithfulness around elaborate meals.

Read Leviticus 23:42-43 and Deuteronomy 16:13-17.

What were the people promised to have in Deuteronomy 16:15?

> **PERSONAL REFLECTION** Describe a time in your past when God sustained you during a wilderness experience. How can you celebrate it, or at least remember that event? It may be doing something as simple as escaping to your favorite chair with your journal and remembering that time with the Lord.

A brief sketch of these three Jewish festivals shows us that God's people have been celebrating His faithfulness together for thousands of years. Each respective festival reminded the Israelites of their liberation, their chosenness, and God's sustaining goodness. In Jesus, we can celebrate these realities in truer and fuller ways.

In the New Testament, we're not explicitly told to keep any feasts beyond communion. And yet, with the coming of Christ and the birth of His church, the people of God are now the family of God. And families don't have to be told to celebrate. They do so naturally because they love each other and especially love the One who made them a family.

As we turn our attention to the New Testament, we will see that the Jewish holidays of the Old Testament are no longer prescribed for followers of Christ—they have been fulfilled in Him. The body of Christ can now celebrate at any time and in any place—the most significant celebration being the weekly gathering of the church. Yearly feasts were incredible, but regular community in Christ is better. The party can now be cued anytime believers are present with one another celebrating the shared life of Christ.

Read Acts 2:42-47. This passage describes what was happening in the early church following the Spirit's coming at Pentecost (another name for Festival of Weeks). Just as the giving of the Law was accompanied by signs and wonders, now the new covenant through Christ is accompanied by the giving of the Holy Spirit![18]

> **PERSONAL REFLECTION** What do you long to experience more of from this celebratory passage, and why?

Read Hebrews 10:24-25.

> **PERSONAL TAKE** The author of Hebrews told us to consider ways we can encourage each other and not neglect gathering together. Why do you think mutual encouragement and physically being present with one another is so vital to our faith?

Read Romans 1:11-12.

What did Paul long for in this passage, and why?

Some of my favorite times of celebration are ones full of mutual encouragement around a table. My friends know me as the queen of soup, which is a rather sad title when one thinks of all the subjects one could be queen of. However, my ability to pull homemade soup out of my fridge for a last-minute gathering is impressive. If our definition of Christian celebration is enjoying being around the shared life of Christ with other believers, even something as simple as soup will do the trick.

> **PERSONAL REFLECTION** What are your favorite ways to celebrate the Lord with others? (Remember, something elaborate isn't necessarily the goal, rather joy and consistency.)

We could look at so many other passages about joy, encouragement, singing, hospitality, and sharing meals, all of which contribute to celebration in their own ways. (If you have the time and want to meditate on additional passages, here are some optional references: John 15:9-10; Gal. 6:10; Eph. 5:18-21; Col. 3:16; Philem. 7; 1 John 1:3; 2 John 1:12.) For now, we'll end with a beloved passage from Luke's Gospel—the parable we often refer to as the prodigal son. This story can be viewed from various theological angles, but today we'll be looking at it solely from the perspective of celebration.

Read Luke 15:11-31. Jesus shared this parable in connection with two others—all three dealing with the joy that comes from finding what was lost.

Why did the father insist on celebrating with the most prized calf, the signet ring, and the best robe (vv. 22-24)?

Verse 24 says they began to _____.

When the older son adamantly contested the lavish celebration for his undeserving brother, what did the father say they had to do, and why?

Scholar Robert Stein pointed out that when the father said they "had to celebrate," the literal meaning is "it was necessary."[19] Stein also noted that this indicates a divine necessary, which is even more remarkable.[20] In other words, "God requires his people to rejoice that salvation is coming to the outcasts."[21] All those Old Testament feasts would eventually find their culmination in Jesus, the One who would gather to Himself all tribes, tongues, men, women, children, Jews, Gentiles—anyone willing to come home to Him. This is worthy of joyous, repeated celebration.

PERSONAL REFLECTION What impacted you the most from today's study on the spiritual practice of celebration, and why?

PERSONAL RESPONSE What intentional step can you take (simple or elaborate) to celebrate the things of God more intentionally with other believers?

Richard Foster put it perfectly, "When the poor receive the good news, when the captives are released, when the blind receive their sight, when the oppressed are liberated, who can withhold the shout of jubilee?"[22]

We're officially halfway through *Encountering God*. I say we celebrate! (See what I did there?) My hope is that the spirit of celebration will infuse the rest of our study of the spiritual disciplines because joy is the hope of them all.

Worship, Fasting, Thanksgiving, and Celebration

WORSHIP

We learned in this session of study that personal and corporate worship can involve expressions of:

- physical posture, such as kneeling, standing, sitting, and even lying face-down before the Lord.

- physical action, such as singing, raising your hands, clapping, dancing, and sitting in reverent silence.

While our physical expression of worship shouldn't be to draw attention to ourselves, like anything in life, excitement and passion are contagious. I'm always inspired by genuine worshipers around me. Collective praise is a joy to be part of.

And when I'm by myself, sometimes I'll pull out my guitar and sing hymns to the Lord, pray words of praise and thanksgiving, read a psalm of praise out loud, or sing along to my favorite worship songs in my playlist.

It's also important to keep in mind that if our lives are surrendered to God and we are walking in His ways to glorify Him, everything we do is an expression of worship to Him.

FASTING

If you've never fasted before, here are some things to keep in mind:

Start small. Maybe fast for one meal. Eat breakfast and dinner, but skip lunch and use your lunch time to spend in prayer and meditation on Scripture.

- Try a 24-hour fast, say from sundown to sundown. Schedule it and possibly ask a friend or small group to join you for accountability, encouragement, and support.

- If you have any health issues, make sure your doctor approves of you fasting.

- If fasting is a trigger for past eating disorders, simply abstain from something else besides food.

THANKSGIVING

Expressing your thanks should be a normal, consistent part of your prayer life. But also:

- Find specific times to spend in thanksgiving (besides on the fourth Thursday of November).

- Keep an ongoing list in your journal of what you're thankful for and add to it occasionally or at specific times.

- Keep a list of specific areas of thanksgiving—spiritual blessings, physical, material, financial, and relationships.

- When you're with your friends, ask them what they're thankful for. One of my friends and I do this every so often on walks. Especially if I'm being negative, we'll change the topic of conversation and talk about what we're grateful to the Lord for.

CELEBRATION

Regular celebration of who God is and what God has done can be practiced:

- in your personal time with the Lord. Sometimes I'll set aside time with the Lord that's more relaxing and less structured than some of the other spiritual disciplines I practice. I'll take a walk, make dinner, work in my garden, or sit with a cup of tea and reflect. It may not look like a wild party, but it's my way of celebrating life with the Lord.

- with the body of Christ in corporate worship, but also over fun dinners, at milestone gatherings, and on certain meaningful occasions.

- around the table—gather friends and celebrate God's blessings as you eat together.

WATCH SESSION FOUR VIDEO

DISCUSSION QUESTIONS

What's something that really stood out to you in the video teaching?

How would you describe what it means to worship God?

How does self-sufficiency hinder our worship? When have you experienced this?

How is it possible for us to worship out of our pain? When has this been your experience?

Why do we sometimes get lost in the trappings of worship—the right place, the right time, the best music, and so forth—and miss the heart of what worship is all about?

What do you think it means to be a passionate worshiper? Would you consider yourself to be one? Why or why not?

How do cultural norms affect how you express your worship to the Lord?

The woman who anointed Jesus worshiped with what she had. What specifically do you have to bring to Jesus as part of your worship of Him? And how does being forgiven much inspire you to love Him much?

What does it mean to worship the Lord with our possessions? Why is it so important we do so, and how are you currently doing that?

Video sessions available for purchase or rent at lifeway.com/encounteringgod

SESSION FIVE

Quiet

JOURNALING THE SESSION

Use this page throughout your session of study. We've given you some prompts, but feel free to write other thoughts and questions to help you learn and process the spiritual disciplines of meditation, remembrance, and solitude.

PREPARING FOR THE SESSION

Before you start your work this session, journal some of your thoughts about the disciplines of meditation, remembrance, and solitude. How have you practiced these disciplines in the past? What has hindered your practice of these disciplines? What do you hope to get out of this session?

DURING THE SESSION

What are some key things you're learning this session about the disciplines of meditation, remembrance, and solitude?

REVIEWING THE SESSION

What are your biggest takeaways from this session, and how will you put them into practice?

Session Five Introduction

Two of my friends bought spiffed up exercise bikes. The kind with screens and classes taught by absurdly fit instructors. They shouldered the big investment; I purchased the click-in shoes. This is called opportunism, my friends. While burning calories, I've picked up a lot of new terminology from the coaches. One of my favorite phrases is *active recovery*. I typically enter the active recovery phase after the instructor has brought me to a point just shy of death and before the next big cardio push. During this phase, I catch my breath, hydrate, and slow down my cycling pace. But I don't stop. Goodness, they don't let you stop. I keep the pedals moving and actively recover, hence the phrase.

When I think of this session's spiritual disciplines (meditation, remembrance, and solitude), I can't think of a better way to describe them than disciplines of active recovery. After the big pushes of thoughtful Bible study, devoted prayer times, worship, and fasting, this session's disciplines allow us to catch our spiritual, mental, and emotional breath. For instance, meditating on Scripture is the quiet enjoyment of God through His Word. Remembrance allows us to pause as we reflect on God's faithfulness in times past. And solitude calls us away from the deafening cacophony of busyness so we can hear His voice.

All of these disciplines are distinct, yet they complement one another. Solitude enhances Scripture meditation; Scripture meditation enriches our remembrance of God's works, and meaningful remembrance encourages us toward time alone with the Lord. Though the disciplines of solitude, remembrance, and meditation are naturally more restful, they aren't idle activities. We will continue to turn the pedals but at a slower and more thoughtful pace and with a different goal in mind. We're not trying to produce or achieve; rather we're seeking restoration, renewal, and refreshment in the presence of Jesus.

If we're used to finding our identity and fulfillment by incessant activity—even "good" busyness—this session's practices will at first be challenging. We might feel like we need to be doing something, for goodness sake. After all, we live in the land of productivity, people! We may also avoid these practices because we're dyed-in-the-wool extroverts who need people and activity—otherwise oxygen might not get to our brains. But before productivity and people comes preparation. As Dallas Willard pointed out in his book, *The Spirit of the Disciplines*, "Just try fasting, prayer, service, giving, or even celebration without the preparation accomplished in withdrawal . . ."[1]

Our lives are indeed meant to bear everlasting fruit, to be productive, but this production ironically springs from spending time with Jesus and abiding in Him (John 15:5,16). This is a difficult concept for those of us who have grown up in spiritual environments that emphasize or reward a lot of Christian activity, especially what can be visibly measured. Of course, our Christian faith calls for doing and activity, but not at the expense of punctuated pauses with our Savior. Ironically, as we abide in Christ through the "active recovery disciplines," we can't help but produce fruit. Jesus explained it like this, "I am the vine; you are the branches. The one who remains in me and I in him

> As we move toward the rambling brooks of Scripture meditation, the still waters of remembrance, and solitude's crisp air, we do so to meet with our Savior.

produces much fruit, because you can do nothing without me" (John 15:5). In the oddest way, more kingdom-productivity may require less frenzied activity.

The quiet and reflective spiritual disciplines that help us abide in Christ surprisingly take practice. Distractors are ever-present. We're addicted to noise, activity, and, dare I say, our personal devices. This is why the spiritual disciplines that require silence and reflection will most likely cause discomfort in the beginning. Our minds will wander. We'll wonder how many text messages we're missing. We will feel an overwhelming need to see if our friend who threw the big dinner party last night has posted pictures yet—did the color of my turtle-neck pop? We will think of all the things we need to do—we have so much to do! It is then we can remind ourselves of Paul's prayer for the Ephesians that they would be strengthened in their inner beings, not in their ability to up production (Eph. 3:16).

On the other hand, you may long for quiet and reflection, yet you find yourself avoiding it because you're saddled with fear or grief. Or you're harboring shame you don't know what to do with. The stillness allows for these uncomfortable thoughts to surface, so our instinct is to keep them at bay with noise. Or maybe you can't pinpoint any specific pain or problem in your life, but in pulling away by yourself, you unearth a vague loneliness or sense of dissatisfaction you can't put your finger on. Ah, yes, meditating on Scripture and withdrawing to silence uncovers what's really happening in the deep places of our souls. But, praise the Lord, He doesn't leave us alone in our struggles. Jesus personally invites us to His side: "Come to me, all of you who are weary and burdened, and I will give you rest" (Matt. 11:28.) The process of quieting our lives may feel unsettling at first, but this is the first step toward peace, rest, and flourishing at the ground level of our souls.

This session, as we move toward the rambling brooks of Scripture meditation, the still waters of remembrance, and solitude's crisp air, we do so to meet with our Savior. We engage in these disciplines because they put us in the best position to hear from God long enough for the Word to do its work in us. Then, when we reenter "life" and relationships, we'll do so with deeper peace and more to offer. We won't be gasping for air with nothing to give those around us. We will have drunk deeply from the Lord and addressed what keeps us at bay from His presence. We will have actively recovered.

Reflecting on God's Word

Time lost can never be retrieved. Time cannot be hoarded, only spent well.[2]

J. OSWALD SANDERS

The word *meditation* can throw us off because it's often attached to Eastern practices of emptying one's mind or detaching from the physical world. But the Christian discipline of meditating on Scripture is about filling our minds with Scripture, truth, and the Holy Spirit.[3] It's not about detaching but about holding fast to Jesus. The strongest argument for Scripture meditation is that the practice is rooted in the Bible itself. God told Joshua to meditate on His law day and night (Josh. 1:8). The psalmist delighted in meditating on God's instruction (Ps. 119:97), and James wrote about looking intently into the Scriptures as one looks into a mirror (Jas. 1:23-25).

Bible study and Scripture meditation have overlapping qualities but are two distinct disciplines. Studying the Bible may include actions like researching context, authorship, and cultural surroundings, cross-referencing, and examining commentaries and word studies. Scripture meditation sets those activities aside for a slow and reflective reading of a small passage. It focuses more on the question, *What does the Holy Spirit want to say to me?*

Meditation on a small passage of Scripture helps us go deep versus wide. It's quality over quantity. We will ask questions of the passage, but we won't immediately run to outside resources for answers. We'll think deeply about certain words and phrases that spring to the forefront and linger in the message of the text. When we're moved by an insight, lament, or delightful truth, we'll naturally want to respond in prayer and worship. I also like to have a pen and journal on hand when meditating on Scripture because the treasures to be gained are too good not to be kept and remembered.

Christian meditation has been defined in different ways, but for this study's purposes, I'll describe it this way: Unhurried time spent reflecting on a small portion of Scripture for the purpose of hearing from God and responding to His voice. Here are a few other helpful definitions: Donald Whitney described meditation as ". . . deep thinking on the truths and spiritual realities revealed in Scripture . . . for the purposes of understanding, application, and prayer."[4] Dallas Willard wrote that meditation is when ". . . we withdraw into silence where we prayerfully and steadily focus upon [the Word]."[5] I also like the way Richard Foster differentiates meditation from study: "Whereas the study of Scripture centers on exegesis, the meditation of Scripture centers on internalizing and personalizing the passage."[6] That our meditation sits upon the foundation of a sound understanding of Scripture is assumed.

Today we'll set the biblical precedent for meditation, and tomorrow we'll practice it. Before we begin looking at different passages, it's helpful to know that the Bible refers to three general objects of meditation: Scripture itself, God's works, and God's attributes as revealed in Scripture.[7] Most of the Bible's references to meditation in the Old Testament have to do with reflecting on God's Law or instruction—His revealed words to us. But we also read about the psalmist dwelling deeply on God Himself and His attributes or rehearsing His actions from days gone by.

Look up the following verses and answer the corresponding questions below. Since we're emphasizing slow reflection, take your time. Also, next to each reference in the space provided, write the words *God's Word*, *God's Works*, or *God's Character*, depending on what the object of meditation is. But don't get so hung up on determining the correct category that you miss the message. The content is most important.

Psalm 1:1-3 _____

The person who meditates on the Lord's instruction is like what? Answer in your own words.

Psalm 63:1-8 _____

What reason did the psalmist give for meditating on God during the night watches?

Psalm 119:97-104 _____

How much of the day did the psalmist meditate on the Lord's instruction (v. 97)? (Circle the correct answer.)

During Bible study   On Sunday morning   All day long   On the weekend

---

PERSONAL REFLECTION Do you find that God's ways and instructions are in your thoughts throughout the day, or do they seem separate from "real life"? Explain your answer.

PERSONAL TAKE We have a tendency to think of God's instruction as laborious or dry. But the psalmist described God's commands as sweeter than honey. Why do you think he used this strong metaphor (vv. 103-104)?

Psalm 77:7-12 and Psalm 143:1-6 _____

What do both psalmists do in Psalm 77:11-12 (Asaph) and Psalm 143:5 (David)?

PERSONAL REFLECTION How does meditating on God's past works bring you hope during suffering and trials?

I want to look at one more integral example of meditating on God's Word. As the Israelites were preparing to cross the Jordan that separated the wilderness from the promised land, the Lord gave specific instructions to their new leader, Joshua. When we consider all the things the Lord could have spoken to him—military instruction, leadership reminders, tips on cultivating a new land— what God said to Joshua might surprise you.

Read Joshua 1:6-9.

What did God tell Joshua to do day and night?

(Circle the correct answer.) God told Joshua to meditate on God's Law so he could:

Observe/do it   Have more Bible knowledge   Appear holy   Earn favor with God

What was promised to Joshua if he meditated on and lived out God's instruction (vv. 7-8)?

In verse 8, the word *meditate* can also mean *recite*.[8] Joshua was to reflect so deeply on God's words that they would lodge in his memory, ready to be recited at any moment. This makes sense because when you're memorizing a passage, you can't help but meditate on it. And better understanding a passage helps you memorize it. I memorized Colossians 1:15-20. This hymn has a ton of prepositions about Jesus, some of which I kept mistakenly interchanging. I had to think closely about what each small preposition meant in order to memorize the passage word for word. Having to think about the meaning of each word resulted in me more deeply meditating on Christ and His attributes. Point being, God desires His people to know His Word inside and out, so much so that it will always be on our lips—ever present, pouring out of us because it is in us.

> **PERSONAL REFLECTION** What truth or realization from today's study helped you recognize the importance of taking time to meditate on Scripture? Describe it. Don't worry if you're still not sure what Scripture meditation looks like exactly. We'll take those practical steps tomorrow. For now, reflect on its importance as revealed in Scripture.

It's no surprise that most uses of the word *meditate* are found in the Book of Psalms. The very essence of the Psalms is reflective, poetic, and thoughtful. The Psalms are nothing if not intimate expressions of God's people longing for and communing with Him. And they're as relevant to our modern lives as they were to the people of the day in which they were penned.

As we continue this session's study on some of the more reflective disciplines, get ready to settle into your favorite chair with your best cup of tea. Or make plans to walk your favorite route through the woods. Find your pen and journal. We'll keep turning the pedals, but we'll be refreshed as we meditate, remember, and listen.

The Best Portion

Silence is nothing else but waiting for God's Word and coming from God's Word with a blessing.[9]

DIETRICH BONHOEFFER

Often in our rush to find out what someone else thinks about a passage of Scripture, we miss what God wants to say to us. If Bible study is mining for gold, Scripture meditation is admiring and reflecting on the gold's beauty. Writing this study has made me realize that I don't meditate on Scripture as much as I used to. As I consider what has contributed to this decline, one main reason stands out—busyness.

Since we're in Session Five and pretty much spiritual-disciplines experts at this point, we already know that busyness is spiritual-disciplines-kryptonite. But the problem with busyness is that it can strut through the front door cloaked in noble activities and ministry to-dos, busting up a good thirty minutes with the Lord. It doesn't always look like silly distractions we can easily spot.

Read Luke 10:38-42.

List all the ways Martha was described in verses 40-41.

PERSONAL TAKE Do you think Martha was doing something important and therefore had a good reason for why she wasn't sitting with Mary at Jesus' feet? Explain.

PERSONAL REFLECTION How does being distracted, worried, upset, or busy with reasonable activities become primary obstacles to spending intimate time with Jesus?

What two things did Mary do according to verse 39? Why are both significant?

When we take into account the historical and cultural background of this text, the scene becomes more dramatic. Verse 39 says that Mary "sat at the Lord's feet." This may not strike us as being that out of the ordinary until we realize that the technical meaning of this phrase is "to be a disciple of."[10] Though Jewish women in the ancient world could attend synagogue and learn, it was unheard of for a rabbi to enter a woman's home for the purpose of instructing her.[11] In short, Jesus was inviting Mary into a place of discipleship traditionally reserved for men.

PERSONAL REFLECTION How does the cultural background of this text further your appreciation of Jesus inviting Mary to learn from Him?

Jesus made one of my favorite statements in verse 42. The CSB reads, "but one thing is necessary. Mary has made the right choice, and it will not be taken away from her."

The literal translation of the "right choice" is the "better portion" or the "right meal." In other words, Mary had the opportunity to be a disciple of Jesus', and whatever other portions might be served her that day, nothing was more nourishing than hearing from Him.

Too often I find that the important or urgent gets in the way of the necessary. Occasionally I rush through my time with the Lord because I'd rather scroll social media or eat cake or watch a movie. But most of the time, it's because I have reasonable, important things to do! Like Martha making dinner for Jesus—on second thought, not that important. But Jesus didn't want something from Martha; He wanted something for her. He didn't need her to feed Him; He wanted to feed her. I get this turned around all the time.

PERSONAL REFLECTION Why do we prioritize important activities ahead of necessary time with Jesus? Take some time with this.

Today we'll close by practicing Scripture meditation—sitting at Jesus' feet and listening to what He has to say. Before we do, consider these words from the extraordinary prayer warrior Madame Guyon, "If you read quickly, it will benefit you little. You will be like a bee that merely skims the surface of a flower. Instead . . . you must become as the bee who penetrates into the depths of the flower. You plunge deeply within to remove its deepest nectar."[12]

Scripture Meditation

Turn over to John 15:1-5. You'll read this passage five times, and after each reading, we'll ask questions of the text. Before you begin, ask the Holy Spirit to speak to you through this passage. Give Him any cares or distractions. Maybe envision yourself sitting at Jesus' feet like Mary receiving a portion for the day.

Read John 15:1-5.

AFTER FIRST READING	In a few sentences, what do you think was Jesus' main point?	
AFTER SECOND READING	Write down all the metaphors Jesus used. Why do you think He used these particular agricultural metaphors? How do metaphors help us understand deep spiritual truths?	
AFTER THIRD READING	Describe what you discovered in this third reading that you didn't notice the first two times.	
AFTER FOURTH READING	Is there a particular word or phrase that stands out to you in the text? If so, what is it, and why is it resonating with you?	
AFTER FIFTH READING	How is the Holy Spirit addressing these "standout" words and phrases in your life today? What encouragement, conviction, or revelation is He bringing? Richard Foster said, "Always remember that we enter the story not as passive observers, but as active participants. Also remember that Christ is truly with us to teach us, to heal us, to forgive us."[13]	

PERSONAL REFLECTION Sit for a few minutes with your insights from John 15:1-5. After some quiet reflection, spend time praying the truths of the passage. Feel free to journal additional thoughts about Jesus as the True Vine, ourselves as the branches, and God the Father as the Master Gardener.

Set aside consistent time to sit at the feet of Jesus and listen to what He says.

Hopefully you've tasted enough of Scripture meditation to want to make it a regular part of your spiritual diet. We'll continue to look at this thoughtful discipline tomorrow but with an emphasis on remembrance. Commit to setting aside consistent time to sit at the feet of Jesus and listen to what He says. It's the best portion of the day.

Remembering the Past for Present Strength

It is not by any new revelation that the Spirit comforts. He does so by telling us old things over again. He brings a fresh lamp to manifest the treasures hidden in Scripture. He unlocks the strong chests where the truth had long been, and he points to secret chambers filled with untold riches. However, he mints no new coins, for enough is done. There is enough in the Bible for you to live on forever.[14]

CHARLES H. SPURGEON

Remembrance can be a form of meditation as we reflect on God's works both in Scripture and in our personal lives. Taking a moment to dwell on who God has always been and what He has done gives us strength in the present and hope for the future. This spiritual discipline can be practiced corporately, as believers recount God's faithfulness together and also individually. My hope is that the practice of remembrance will swiftly turn into gratitude as you recall the blessings of the Lord's past works.

For me, sometimes taking the time to remember feels like a needless luxury, especially when all these pressing needs are happening right this very moment. But what I've learned to cherish about remembering God's past faithfulness is how remembrance informs my present and future. I can't see either clearly without having first put on my remembrance spectacles. We'll see why this is true as we look at today's Scripture: Nehemiah 9.

I love this chapter because it shows God's people recounting their history with the Lord. What's especially interesting is that they choose to remember in the middle of hardship. This account takes place not long after the Jewish people had returned from the Babylonian exile to rebuild Jerusalem. They are back in the promised land but still under Persian rule. In fact, it might be a good idea to start with their plight so we can better appreciate their practice of remembrance.

Read Nehemiah 9:36-37.

In your own words, briefly describe the Jews' difficult situation. Detail their concerns.

Now read verses 5-6.

How far back do the Jews "remember" in verses 5-6, and why do you think starting there was important?

I remember seeking help from a professional counselor during a trying time in my life. I can't recall what we were talking about, but about halfway into our conversation I remember him saying, "How about we go back to the beginning." That was my cue to launch into the horrors of kindergarten and my scary teacher with a red perm who made my hands shake while she hovered over me and my abacus. Then I noticed my counselor thumbing to the Book of Genesis, and I realized he was talking about *the* beginning, not my beginning in school. Remembering what God has done in our lifetimes is essential, but even more important is remembering what He did before we came to be. I've never forgotten the significance of that moment when I learned to read my own story in light of God's story.

Continue reading verses 7-15.

What covenant promise did God make with Abraham (then Abram) (v. 8)?

Years after God's covenant with Abraham, what did He do for His people living in bondage in Egypt (v. 11)?

The people of Nehemiah's day recounted three things the Lord did for the Israelites while they walked through the wilderness after their deliverance from Egypt.

1. With a pillar of cloud by day and a pillar of fire by night, God _____ His people (v. 12).

2. When He spoke to them, what did He give them (vv. 13-14)?

3. He provided what two essential elements for His people (v. 15)?

Read verses 16-21.

Not long after God delivered the Israelites from bondage, they turned their backs on Him. Fill in the blank: The people didn't listen, and they didn't _____ God's past works He'd done among them (v. 17).

PERSONAL TAKE What connection do you see between not remembering God's faithfulness in your life and turning your back on Him?

Though Nehemiah and his people continued to recount the rebellion of their forefathers, what consistent attributes of God did they also recount? Look at verses 17-21.

PERSONAL REFLECTION How does God's past compassion, mercy, and kindness give you hope for what feels like a lost cause in your life?

Keep reading verses 22-31. This section briefly details the Israelites' possession of Canaan (the promised land), their exile, and God's continued kindness toward them.

PERSONAL TAKE Knowing the difficult situation the Jews of Nehemiah's day were in, why do you think they chose to recount the major ways God had shown His faithfulness to them and their ancestors?

I sat with a small gathering of twenty-somethings in my living room. We discussed how difficult it is for them in this season of their lives to trust God for a husband, a future family, a career they love, another new roommate. They're right now forging their histories with God and learning His faithfulness. As someone who is just a bit further down the road—and I do mean just a couple of feet ahead (or possibly twenty years)—I shared a few of the times God has proven faithful in my life. I told them God won't always do what they want, but He will do more than they can dream up.

I said these things because I believe in the truth of God's Word. But because of my age, I also said them because I have more history with God to remember. I've logged a little more time with the Lord than they have. I have more past experiences of His faithfulness to draw from. They're making their own future memories with Him now. As God proves His faithfulness to them in the present, they'll have their own stories to remember in future times of trial and joy.

PERSONAL REFLECTION Remembering God's past faithfulness changes the way we approach our present challenges. Write about a significant time God moved in your life in the past and how that encourages you to boldly seek Him in your present circumstances.

We don't have time to trace the theme of remembrance into the New Testament, but it's certainly there. Jesus told His disciples that after His departure, the Holy Spirit would remind them of all Jesus had taught them (John 14:26). Paul told the believers in Corinth to take the Lord's Supper in remembrance of Jesus (1 Cor. 11:23-26). Peter wrote about God's truth waking us up by reminding us of God's truth (2 Pet. 1:12-13; 3:1).

So I hope remembering God's faithfulness is one of the spiritual disciplines you continue to incorporate into your life's rhythms. If you're not sure how to continue, turn to page 138 for a list of passages you can meditate on, along with some helpful guidance. By the time you meditate on all these passages, you'll have some great experience to build on. As the psalmist wrote, over time you will be like a rooted tree planted by flowing streams, bearing fruit in its appointed season, flourishing with lush foliage that will not wither. And whatever you do will prosper (Ps. 1:2-3).

DAY 4 — *Abundance in the Desert*

SOLITUDE

Only in the fellowship do we learn to be rightly alone and only in aloneness do we learn to live rightly in the fellowship.[15]

DIETRICH BONHOEFFER

Solitude. We have so little of it in our culture. Friends of mine who are mothers tell me of locking themselves in the bathroom away from their toddlers and teenagers to capture three quiet minutes. Susanna Wesley, mother of John Wesley who founded the Methodist church, used to enter into solitude by pulling her apron over her head.[16] She could pitch a prayer tent just like that. This is what I like to call *resourceful.* On the other hand, we've probably also experienced the sheer terror of too much alone time. If things get overly quiet, we start to get antsy.

I went through a deeply lonely time during my first few years in Nashville. My big weekly outings were trips to the grocery store. I knew very few people and had almost no community I could count on. To this day I enjoy alone time, but I don't like it forced upon me. I don't like to be abandoned into it. Occasionally, the underlying fear of solitude turning into loneliness can keep me from choosing time alone over community when both are offered—even when a span of quiet is the more needful option.

Whether we're afflicted with a terrible case of FOMO (fear of missing out) or we're afraid to be alone with our thoughts, fears, regrets, or questions, it seems we have this love-hate relationship with solitude. We simultaneously crave and fear it. We want alone time up to the point of it feeling downright unsettling. And often, when we finally have it, we have an overwhelming urge to fill it: music, podcasts, social media, folding laundry, watching a show. What will we discover if it's just us and God?

As we think about solitude from a Christian perspective, its purpose is to clear space for drawing closer to God, not to just be by ourselves. When we choose silence and aloneness, we do so in order to lay aside distractions to better hear from and commune with God. Ironically, we choose to be alone so we can be with Him. Today and tomorrow we'll look at how Jesus prized solitude when He walked on earth. By doing so, we'll also discover how much we need it.

Before we begin, let's do a short self-assessment. Put a mark on the following spectrum that best identifies your comfort with silence and solitude.

SOLITUDE

Extremely uncomfortable   Comfortable

PERSONAL REFLECTION (RESPOND TO BOTH)

Why do you crave solitude? List every reason you can think of.

Why do you avoid solitude? List every reason you can think of.

Read Luke 5:15-16.

PERSONAL TAKE The CSB says Jesus often withdrew to deserted places. What does this tell us about the value Jesus placed on solitude?

Read Mark 6:30-32.

True/False: The disciples reported to Jesus all they'd done and taught.

Where did Jesus invite His disciples to go with Him? And for what purpose?

How did Jesus and His disciples get to the remote place? (Circle the correct answer.)

By foot   By camel   By boat   By donkey

Your translation may say *quiet place, deserted place, desolate place, remote place,* or *solitary place.* The literal translation of the Greek word is simply *wilderness.* It can also mean a "place without inhabitants," where no distraction would separate Jesus or His disciples from God.[17]

PERSONAL REFLECTION What is both inviting and unsettling about being in a place where nothing separates you from God?

When Jesus encouraged His disciples to come away with Him to a remote place, it wasn't so they could grab a bite in peace or even catch a nap—good things, but Jesus had more in mind. At this point, it's essential to note a recurring theme of the Old Testament—God providing rest for His people in the wilderness.[18] To better understand this, look up the following passages and note what God did for His people in the wilderness in each instance. I've given you five references, each one a reminder that the barrenness of the wilderness is often the stage upon which God performs some of His most dramatic acts.

Next to each reference, write what God did in the wilderness.

DEUTERONOMY 1:29-31	
DEUTERONOMY 8:2-3	
DEUTERONOMY 8:15-16	
PSALM 78:15-16	
HOSEA 2:14-15	

Turn back to Mark 6.

As we reenter this scene, we find that this ancient hope of rest that God provided for His people in the wilderness in the Old Testament now finds its fulfillment in Jesus. He is the ultimate rest for the disciples' lives.[19] The disciples didn't need to fear the solitude of the wilderness because they had a special appointment to fellowship with Jesus.

Scholar James R. Edwards wrote, "The first prerequisite of discipleship is being with Jesus (Mk. 3:14)."[20] This is so obvious that it's easy to miss. He continued, "The life of the disciple is not only mission for Jesus but also mission with Jesus."[21]

Look at Mark 6:33-34.

Did Jesus and the disciples end up getting the solitude they were looking for? Why or why not?

One of the things that physical exercise has taught me over the years is that it's possible to put a short amount of time to really good use. If I've got a window of just thirty minutes, I can take a walk, jump on my friend's bike (because remember, I so did not buy my own), work out on my Pilates machine . . . you get the idea. A moment of time that can otherwise go up in smoke scrolling on your phone can be invested in a way that matters. That boat ride ended up being significant for the disciples because they never got the solitude with Jesus they were expecting. That journey to the place of solitude ended up being the place of solitude.

Tomorrow we'll take another look at the important spiritual discipline of solitude. I hope you were encouraged today by the fact that solitude is not something to fear but rather a space to be enjoyed. Yes, we may at first struggle in our alone time with regret, fear, or loneliness. But remember, as children of God, we don't need to fear the deserted places. Christ is the ultimate provision of rest for us in places of solitude. The desert place is no longer aloneness in its strictest sense. It is time communing with Jesus.

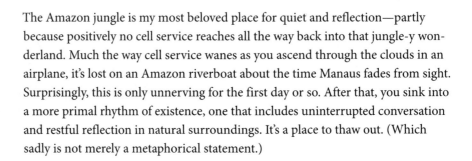

If we give priority to the outer life, our inner life will be dark and scary. We will not know what to do with solitude.[22]

TIM KELLER

The Amazon jungle is my most beloved place for quiet and reflection—partly because positively no cell service reaches all the way back into that jungle-y wonderland. Much the way cell service wanes as you ascend through the clouds in an airplane, it's lost on an Amazon riverboat about the time Manaus fades from sight. Surprisingly, this is only unnerving for the first day or so. After that, you sink into a more primal rhythm of existence, one that includes uninterrupted conversation and restful reflection in natural surroundings. It's a place to thaw out. (Which sadly is not merely a metaphorical statement.)

There are two challenges to falling asleep in a hammock on a riverboat in the Amazon jungle: stifling heat and eerie silence. (That's if you don't count the sleeping in a hammock in the Amazon jungle part.) The unsettling silence can go one of two ways, depending on where your boat is anchored. It's either dead quiet, or you're surrounded by a cacophony of both harmless and we-will-kill-you-if-you-come-near-us nocturnal creatures making known their presence. On one particular noisy night, my sister Katie flipped on a battery powered noise machine to the applause of all the Americans. It was the sleeping pill we needed to drown the noise and lull us to sleep. Everyone was positively thrilled except our Amazonian jungle guide, Milton.

The next morning over eggs and manioc rolls, Milton piped up, "What was that strange noise you guys turned on last night?" We attempted to explain the concept of white noise, which, admittedly, sounded ridiculous. Despite our every effort to justify turning on artificially produced sound for the sake of drowning out natural sound, such as clicking caimans and croaking toads, the problem clearly lay with us, not with Milton. He was the free man in our midst, able to fall sound asleep to any background noise, or lack thereof, except the fabricated one we'd introduced.

While silence and solitude aren't the same thing, they're companions. If we're going to practice more solitude, we need to get more comfortable with silence. Because of our digitally connected world, it's important to be proactive about protecting times of quiet and reflection. Solitude by its very nature should include quiet. In his book on the spiritual disciplines, Donald Whitney wrote, "More than any generation in history we must discipline ourselves to enjoy the blessings of silence and solitude."[23] If this requires effort and practice for you, you're not alone.

Yesterday we read that Jesus often withdrew to deserted places. We learned that the Old Testament theme of God providing for His people in the wilderness found its fulfillment in Jesus as our ultimate provision. We were reminded that while we resist solitude for lots of reasons, it is an essential discipline that recharges, restores, and renews.

Read Matthew 14:1-14.

What tragedy took place (vv. 10-12)? (Circle the correct answer.)

Peter was imprisoned

John the Baptist was beheaded

Paul was persecuted

James was martyred

How did Jesus respond (v. 13)?

Did Jesus get the alone time He was seeking (v. 13)?

> **PERSONAL TAKE** Why do you think Jesus sought alone time with His Father after such a loss? What do you think Jesus wanted from His Father?

We noted yesterday that Jesus didn't initially get the alone time He was seeking when He and His disciples arrived at the deserted place. He didn't seem to get it in this passage either (v. 13). People were constantly tugging on Him. The hungry needed feeding; the sick needed healing; the disciples needed teaching and answers and friendship. This noise and insatiable need from so many reminds us that Jesus' life wasn't naturally suited for silence or solitude. His life was no monastery. He had to intentionally seek out time with the Father, often during inconvenient hours and in inconvenient places. Jesus did so because fellowship with His Father was essential to His life and ministry.

Continue reading verses 15-23.

After sending His disciples ahead and dismissing the crowds, where did Jesus go, and why (v. 23)?

We may not know for sure why Jesus withdrew from the crowds, but my personal opinion is that Jesus needed tending from His Father after such a devastating loss.

PERSONAL REFLECTION What do you seek from the Lord in your alone time with Him when you've had a loss, heartbreak, or trial?

Look back at Matthew 14:13,23. A lot happened between these verses. What does this tell you about Jesus' follow-through in getting that alone time with His Father?

Jesus was persistent in His pursuit of solitude even through interruption. Though the needy crowd initially kept Him from solitude, He kept seeking it until He finally found it.

John Mark Comer said, "In Luke's gospel in particular, you can chart Jesus' life along two axis points: the busier and more in demand and famous Jesus became, and the more he withdrew to his quiet place to pray."[24]

PERSONAL REFLECTION What practical steps can you take to ensure that you balance out a busy day or a particularly busy season with quiet times spent with God?

I want us to visit one more passage about Jesus seeking solitude.

Read John 7:1-10.

This passage begins with Jesus' brothers inviting Him to travel from Galilee to Jerusalem for the Jewish Festival of Booths. They wanted Him to perform impressive miraculous signs to promote His message. They apparently hadn't yet noticed that this is not exactly how Jesus ran His ministry. He told them to go on ahead, and eventually, He followed.

> True/False: Jesus took advantage of journeying to the festival to fellowship with His disciples.

Galilee was ninety miles from Jerusalem, about five days of walking in solitude when traveling between the two locations.[25] We learn a valuable lesson from Jesus here: Jesus didn't make His plans based on what everyone thought He should do but according to the leading of His Father. His brothers pushed Him to go to the festival to show Himself to the world. Jesus would not be persuaded to reveal Himself in that way until the Father's timing had come. D. A. Carson said that Jesus remained in Galilee for a time ". . . because his life is regulated by his heavenly Father's appointments . . ."[26] Well, now, that just zings me.

PERSONAL REFLECTION How do you allow other people's demands or requests to sway you from times of solitude with the Lord?

PERSONAL JOURNAL What do today's Scripture passages teach you about the importance of having regular times of solitude with God? Write about it from every angle you can think of. For instance, how did Jesus plan for solitude? How did He pursue it? Why was it important? Was it always convenient? What types of sacrifices did solitude require?

I want to close with a short text that takes place right before Judas betrayed Jesus. While the main point of this passage is not about having times of solitude with Jesus, a few passing mentions bring this theme to the forefront.

Read John 18:1-2.

What specific place was across the Kidron Valley?

Who did Jesus go there with?

How did Judas know where this place was (v. 2)?

> **PERSONAL TAKE** Why do you think Jesus chose a quiet, out of the way garden to meet regularly with His disciples? What about that setting enhances rest, listening, and fellowship?
>
>
> **PERSONAL REFLECTION** If Jesus met regularly with His disciples in a quiet garden outside of the city, how does this inspire you to capture those times alone with Him whenever possible?

I've found that when I don't carve out time to commune with Jesus, stilling myself before Him and carrying to Him my fears, questions, or burdens, I am tossed about with no enduring anchor. Even if nothing particularly challenging is going on in my life, without silence and solitude to pray and listen to God, I'm more prone to draw from my own well of strength and assumptions. I become me-filled, not Holy Spirit saturated.

Next session we'll be studying the easy-to-overlook disciplines of simplicity, generosity, and rest. In some ways these practical disciplines are the outflow of meditation, remembrance, and solitude, because they can only be practiced from a place of surrender. Session Six is one of my favorites of the whole study because we get to take an earnest look at what living from a place of soul-rest looks like.

Meditation, Remembrance, and Solitude

MEDITATION

Meditating on Scripture is a practice that happens best when you can plan for it. It's as simple as setting aside a certain amount of time and choosing a short passage to reflect on. You can make Scripture meditation a regular part of your quiet time with the Lord or practice it on the weekends when you may have more time. Here are a couple of things to consider:

- Choose a key word, phrase, or verse to ponder each time you do regular Bible study. Consider what you learned about that verse and how it applies to your life.

- Make Scripture memory a consistent part of your spiritual life. Choose to meditate on the passages you're memorizing. This will not only strengthen your recall of the verses but will deepen the meaning of those passages as well.

If you need help getting started, here's a helpful exercise: Choose one of the following fifteen selections. It doesn't really matter which one you choose. The prize will be in the time you commit to meditate on the passage.

Genesis 1:26-2	Deuteronomy 6:4-9	Joshua 1:6-9	Daniel 2:20-23	Psalm 95:1-7
Psalm 139:13-16	Isaiah 53:4-6	Jeremiah 31:31-34	John 13:12-17	2 Corinthians 10:3-6
Ephesians 3:16-19	Colossians 3:12-15	Hebrews 9:11-14	1 Peter 4:7-11	1 John 5:1-4

Write your passage selection here: _____.

Commit to 20–30 minutes (or more) of undistracted time with God and this passage. Ask the Holy Spirit to speak to you, perhaps using the psalmist's prayer in Psalm 119:18: "Open my eyes so that I may contemplate wondrous things from your instruction." Also, if you get stuck in your time of meditation, consider walking through the questions below by Donald Whitney.

Does this text reveal something I should: *Believe about God? Praise or thank or trust God for? Pray about for myself or others? Have a new attitude about? Make a decision about? Do for the sake of Christ, others, or myself?*[27]

REMEMBRANCE

One exercise to help you with this practice is to do a timeline of your life. Mark on the timeline significant events and situations that have altered the trajectory of your life. Note how God was present in each of those moments:

- How He guided your decisions;

- How He changed your direction;

- How He rescued you from a bad or dangerous situation;

- How He restored you after wrong choices;

- How He blessed you with abundance;

- How He taught you or disciplined you;

- How He refined your character and faith.

This is also an exercise you can do with your family or close friends.

Keeping a journal will also aid you in this discipline. Keep an ongoing account of how the Lord is working in your life. Then periodically take time to look back at how He has been constantly at work in your life through the days, months, and years.

SOLITUDE

All of us, including our favorite extroverts, need some alone time. We need quiet reflective moments where we allow God to still our hearts and minds. Sometimes just letting my mind wander while intentionally being quiet in the presence of God is some of the most restorative time I have.

Here are some keys to practicing this discipline:

- **Schedule it.** Our rushing world usually doesn't afford us much time to spontaneously pull away for a few hours by ourselves.

- **Honor the schedule.** Make it a priority and don't allow the urgent to interrupt the important.

- **Remove distractions.** Put your devices away. If you need to keep it with you for safety reasons, silence it so that you're not constantly interrupted with dings, rings, and other alerts. I can barely pick up my phone without checking Instagram® or the news. I do better when I can't see it.

- **Designate a place.** It can be at a friend's house, a neighbor's quiet porch, a park under a tree, or even a walk you take by yourself. Choosing a spot that's quiet and less trafficked makes it more likely you will be able to be still. Make sure to choose a safe place.

WATCH SESSION FIVE VIDEO

DISCUSSION QUESTIONS

What's something that really stood out to you in the video teaching?

Why are solitude and quiet so important to our spiritual lives? How does our current culture hinder us in this practice?

What is your favorite way, place, and time to draw away and be quiet before the Lord?

How would you define Scripture meditation? Has this been a consistent discipline in your life? Explain.

Why is it important that we draw life from God, not from activity? How do the inner spiritual disciplines like solitude, rest, and Scripture meditation help us do that?

How has your meditation of Scripture helped you in times of difficulty? In times of temptation?

How does busyness get in our way of delighting in and meditating on God's Word? How do our devices do the same? What intentional steps can we take to remove these hindrances?

Kelly talked about the jungle guide who spotted a sloth because he was familiar with the scenery. As your eyes have adjusted to the landscape of Scripture, what wondrous things out of God's law have you recently seen?

Would you say you're living the blessed life as described in Psalm 1? If so, what is the evidence? If not, what changes need to be made?

Video sessions available for purchase or rent
at lifeway.com/encounteringgod

SESSION SIX

Simplify

JOURNALING THE SESSION

Use this page throughout your session of study. We've given you some prompts, but feel free to write other thoughts and questions to help you learn and process the spiritual disciplines of simplicity, generosity, and rest.

PREPARING FOR THE SESSION

Before you start your work this session, journal some of your thoughts about the disciplines of simplicity, generosity, and rest. How have you practiced these disciplines in the past? What has hindered your practice of these disciplines? What do you hope to get out of this session?

DURING THE SESSION

What are some key things you're learning this session about the disciplines of simplicity, generosity, and rest?

REVIEWING THE SESSION

What are your biggest takeaways from this session, and how will you put them into practice?

Session Six Introduction

I lived the first several years of my adult life rather simply. This was not by design but necessity. I have tax records in my basement that verify that season, one in particular documenting an extraordinarily low income. With such a paltry amount, I paid my $430 a month mortgage. I then bought food, clothes, and gas. I tithed what I could. The idea of a savings account was preposterous. Once, someone rammed into my decrepit Jeep, and instead of spending the money the person gave me for repairs, I got to live for another month. This happened twice. Some people are blessed with new cars; I was blessed when people barreled into mine.

It felt odd when I began to make any money to speak of. I suddenly had options I hadn't had before. Do I save more, give more, invest, accumulate stuff, travel, upsize? These were novel choices for me, far from limitless, but choices nonetheless. A few years into a halfway stable career as a writer and speaker, I bought a house. Several years after that, I decided to renovate my kitchen. I cried when I took out the loan. It hadn't been all that long since first being in a position to buy a home; now I was considering renovating what I'd bought. This prospect was not lost on me.

Now, let me just say that if you're looking to simplify your life, under no circumstances undergo a home renovation, especially your kitchen. You will break down into a heap over things as insignificant as backsplash tile and the metal finish of your fixtures. I could have learned Portuguese in the time I spent researching unlacquered brass. When my nephew, Will, who was five years old at the time, tottered into my decimated kitchen, he astutely asked, "So . . . where are we supposed to get our juice?" In other words, "We had what we needed before all this; why have you chosen to put us in such a perilous position?" I could

not for the life of me provide an adequate explanation.

To be fair, I'm grateful for my updated kitchen. It has served as a nourishing space for my family and friends. I enjoy pulling up to the kitchen island even when I'm by myself. But never has *complicated* been more on display than during that renovation. I learned that our consumer culture isn't simply about us consuming its wares but its wares consuming us. And the system in place doesn't just consume our money but also our time. We rationalize: *I've got the money so I might as well buy it or build it.* But do we have the time? Buying more stuff, planning elaborate trips, obsessing over the stock market, caring for multiple homes, forever upgrading to the latest model car, fridge, microwave, phone, mattress—oh my goodness, the amount of mattresses!—requires so much of our God-given time and energy. And how we use that time is either an eternal investment or one without return.

Israel's great leader, Moses, who had experienced everything from the height of Egyptian wealth and luxury to the barrenness of the wilderness, cried to the Lord in Psalm 90:12, "Teach us to number our days carefully so that we may develop wisdom in our hearts." When we reflect on the temporal nature of our lives, we wisely reflect on the use of our time in light of that reality. Numbering our days isn't figuring out how many we have. It's living them lean and mean in light of how limited they are. The spiritual discipline of simplicity helps free us to live our days fully devoted to the Lord, so nothing

> When we reflect on the temporal nature of our lives, we wisely reflect on the use of our time in light of that reality.

hinders us from investing our time and money into what's eternal. The simpler we live, the freer we live. The more we deliberately pare back, the less encumbered we are to live for the Lord and others in the present moment—the only one we're guaranteed.

Over the years I've found that simplicity runs in and out of several of the other disciplines. Simplicity is a tributary to the larger body of water we call rest. It's nearly impossible to Sabbath when the choppy waves of over-commitment and material attachments are working against us. Yet while sailing with the current of simplicity and Sabbath, we naturally glide into generosity. When we're uninhibited by unnecessary cares and duly refreshed by a day with the Lord, our time, resources, and very beings are available to those who need us. This way of life is not an impossibility. Neither should a hint of legalism or self-righteousness accompany its path. We don't exchange stuff for piousness but for a life of meaning.

While we often think of a lifestyle of simplicity, Sabbath, and generosity as characterized by having less and missing out on more, the opposite is true when our goal is to experience more of Jesus. These disciplines in particular free us to experience the fullness of life in the kingdom of God! We practice them because we long for something so much grander than a big purchase that doesn't deliver happiness, a dream job that robs us of rest, or feeling miserly when we have little to give because everything's "tied up." When we're unencumbered from more stuff, we're suddenly nimble enough to be available to the Lord in ways we couldn't have imagined.

The tendency is to think this type of lifestyle is for super holy, exceptional Christians. For missionary types. You know, the ones with a "calling." Or we think that all this sounds laudable but entirely unattainable. That's why I'm so excited for this session and the practice of these spiritual disciplines. We'll take it step by step because we won't get there overnight. We won't wake up tomorrow suddenly free of our Pinterest® obsessions or stock market addictions. Hence, we will practice these disciplines that, little by little, grace upon grace, will lead us into what Jesus described as the abundant life.

Living Without Hindrance

Desire one thing: God's presence. And you will be less driven by all those phony desires that matter not at all.[1]

WALTER BRUEGGEMANN

I love the idea of arranging our lives around what matters most and excluding what doesn't contribute to Christ's purposes.[2] Jesus told us through His Word what those vital purposes are. And when we need specific instruction that might not be expressly addressed in Scripture, we rely on the Holy Spirit to reveal what the practical arrangements of life should look like in different seasons and circumstances.

When it comes to the spiritual discipline of simplicity in American culture, most of our lives are so overgrown with the vines of materialism and entitlement that we aren't even aware of the ways we're being choked by an overcomplicated way of life. I don't want to saddle us with guilt, but I don't want to remove conviction either. The Holy Spirit will help us decipher between the two. So I encourage you to begin this session's study with a time of prayer and surrender to the Lord's leading. Only through the Spirit's prodding and our obedience to Him will we find freedom from an anxious, discontented, overly busy life.

> **PERSONAL PRAYER** Pause to quiet yourself before God. Share with Him your honest feelings about this idea of simplicity. Confess your attachments to the things of this world. (We all have them!) Ask Him to show you pictures of freedom and peace as you open His Word today. Or sit quietly in His presence, palms open in humility and expectation as you ask Him to speak to you through this session's study. (Feel free to journal your prayer in the space provided.)

Today we'll look at a few people in Scripture, including Jesus, who lived simply so they could live fully. Before we read today's Scripture passages, note that the selections I've chosen aren't necessarily prescriptions for how we should live but descriptions of how Jesus and His followers lived. Though these passages have much to say to us today and may convict us to make radical changes in our lives, they are not commands. Those will come tomorrow—because I know you were hoping for some.

Read Matthew 8:18-20.

Why do you think Jesus not having a permanent place to lay His head was important to His ministry? It may help to think of the question in reverse: How would Jesus owning a permanent home have affected His ministry?

Read Matthew 10:1-10.

What did the disciples' mission consist of (vv. 1,6-8)?

Why did Jesus tell His disciples to freely give (v. 8)?

PERSONAL TAKE Why do you think Jesus told His disciples not to take money or supplies with them? What would have been the benefit of practicing simplicity in this case?

Read Acts 2:42-47.

What experiences and activities gave the early church deep joy even as they lived modestly? List everything you can find.

Read Hebrews 11:23-27.

Why did Moses demonstrate simplicity for the sake of Christ instead of clinging to the opulent life of Egyptian royalty?

PERSONAL REFLECTION As you consider Jesus, His disciples, the early church, and Moses' lifestyle, what stands out to you most about the blessings/benefits and difficulties/sacrifices of simplicity?

We can point to people in both the Old and New Testaments who lived simply for the sake of God's call on their lives. Whether it was Moses who valued identifying with God's people over the pleasures of Egypt, the early church who thrived in fellowship and the presence of the Holy Spirit instead of their material possessions, or Jesus who lived simply so He could live fully available to His heavenly Father, the principle of living unencumbered for the sake of seeking God's kingdom is one we're all invited to embrace.

Let's look at one of my favorite examples of someone who simplified his life for the greater purpose of accomplishing the work to which God had called him.

Read Nehemiah 5:14-19. In this passage, Nehemiah, governor of Judah, explained his devotion to God versus demanding his rightful privileges.

How did Nehemiah practice the spiritual discipline of simplicity?

Why did he choose not to eat the food allotted to the governor? Give all the reasons you can find.

Living simply isn't only about showing restraint when it comes to having or spending money. It's uncomplicating our lives by paring back anything that saddles us with needless busyness, worry, or stress. I added the word *needless* because in this life we will have stress. But so much of the stress we experience is not a result of eternal endeavors but frivolous ones. Simplifying is decluttering our lives so we're free to serve the Lord and others in whatever capacity He calls us.

I was reminded of this truth on a quiet morning while finishing my read through the Book of Acts. The last two verses say, "Paul stayed two whole years in his own rented house. And he welcomed all who visited him, proclaiming the kingdom of God and teaching about the Lord Jesus Christ with all boldness and *without hindrance*" (Acts 28:30-31, emphasis mine). That phrase *without hindrance* spoke to me.

PERSONAL REFLECTION What areas of your current lifestyle hinder your ability to share the goodness of Jesus or welcome people into your home?

Oftentimes—especially in our affluent and busy culture—simplifying means saying no to what we could do or afford for the sake of the deeper riches and experiences of obedience to God. Along the lines of the apostle Paul's lifestyle, my prayer is that we'd be free to welcome people into our homes and share the life of Jesus without hindrance. Practicing the spiritual discipline of simplicity is a means to an end—the end being an unfettered life that's free to come or go, do or stop, serve or rest when Jesus calls.

A Meaningful Life

Frugality as a settled style of life frees us from indifferent things.[3]

DALLAS WILLARD

The idea of living more simply is not synonymous with living empty. I desperately want that to sink down into your belief bones. When it comes to simplicity, if our focus is on what we're giving up or missing out on, we'll miss the joy of simplifying. When I take my pruning shears to my tomato vines, (assuming I'm keeping up with them), I try not to lament the healthy vines I've lopped and banished to the compost pile. Some of these castoffs even bear tiny green globes. It's a trying discipline, but I prune because the esteemed tomato people tell me that suckers (shoots that sprout between the plant's branch and stem) steal nutrients from the most promising fruit on the tree. So I remove what's good for the promise of what's better: BLT's, caprese salads, Bolognese sauce . . . need I keep going? In spiritual terms, Christian simplicity is doing without certain things so we have more availability for what matters to the heart of Christ, for what brings us abundant life.

> **PERSONAL REFLECTION** How would living more simply in certain areas of your life allow you to live more fully around what's really important?

Yesterday we looked at several characters in Scripture who modeled simplicity. Today we'll explore some passages that instruct us in the ways of simplicity. More of the "how to."

> **PERSONAL REFLECTION** Before we get to the passages, reflect on the following question: *What is the greatest enemy of simplicity in your life?*

I wish I could see what you wrote. You may or may not have touched on the opponents I've considered. Here are four:

1. Love of money and possessions which tends to complicate our lives;

2. Discontentment or boredom that leads to filling our time with the next entertainment, newest experience, or go-to pleasure;

3. Workaholism or overly-busy schedules that complicate our days and keep us from what truly matters;

4. Fear and worry that enslave us by requiring our time, money, and next expensive endeavor to avoid whatever we're afraid might happen.

Today's Scripture passages collectively address all of these issues.

> Christian simplicity is doing without certain things so we have more availability for what matters to the heart of Christ, for what brings us abundant life.

Read 1 Timothy 6:6-14.

According to Paul, godliness plus _____ equals great gain.

> **PERSONAL TAKE** Why do you think being content with the basic necessities of life is especially compatible with godliness?

Read verses 17-19.

Notice that Paul didn't say it's a sin to be wealthy. What two issues did he cite as problematic?

> **PERSONAL TAKE** Look back at verses 11-12,18-19. What does it look like "to be rich in good works" (v. 18)?

Read Hebrews 12:1-2.

What two things did the author of Hebrews tell us we should cast off or lay aside?

The author of Hebrews told us to lay aside every hindrance and sin that easily entangles us and keeps us from running a clean race. This wording means hindrances aren't necessarily sinful by nature but can simply be too much of a good thing—an activity, relationship, or commitment that weighs us down or complicates our mission.

PERSONAL REFLECTION What area(s) of your life do you need to simplify to help you run with more focus and freedom? Remember, this may mean removing a blatant sin, but it can also mean laying something aside that in and of itself is perfectly good for the sake of running the race Jesus has called you to run.

We'll end today by looking at a teaching Jesus gave His disciples about simplicity. And we'll also practice the spiritual discipline of Scripture meditation as we reflect on His teaching. In other words, we'll apply the discipline of Scripture meditation while learning about the discipline of simplicity. If only efficiency were a spiritual discipline.

Slowly read Luke 12:22-34. We tend to think this passage mainly addresses worry and fear, which it certainly does. But it also speaks of a simple and satisfying way of life, characterized by a life of trust in our heavenly Father. Read through it with your simplicity glasses on.

What metaphors and colorful descriptions did Jesus use to describe a simple but full and bountiful life?

What gets in the way of this kind of life? List the obvious answers but also dig for the ones under the surface.

What explicit instruction did Jesus give to combat our anxiety, as well as our hunger for storing up wealth and having the latest and greatest (vv. 31-32)?

What we arrange our lives around tells us what we value most and pursue first. This doesn't mean that seeking God's righteousness and kingdom will look like one enormous Bible study while you eat rice cakes. You'll still find yourself on the soccer field with your child, at your office giving a presentation, at home lost in a gripping novel, or in the kitchen rolling out pizza dough for a dinner party. Yet the activities we choose, the way we invest our time and money, and the motivations we have for everything we do play a part in whether or not we're seeking God's kingdom. Paul said in 1 Corinthians 10:31, "So, whether you eat or drink, or whatever you do, do everything for the glory of God."

PERSONAL REFLECTION Given that caveat, think through what a normal day looks like for you. What parts of your life are arranged in a way that prioritizes Christ and the kingdom of God? And what parts prioritize the cultural values of the world we live in?

It's worth noting that many of the people who first heard Jesus' message were filled with anxiety, not because they had an overabundance of material possessions and wealth but because they had little. They were poor. They worried about their basic needs being met. Many of us deal with the opposite predicament. We are weighed down with the cares and complexities of having too many resources, too many options, too many second opinions, too many possessions to take care of.

Richard Foster wrote, "If, in a comparatively simple society, our Lord lays such strong emphasis upon the spiritual dangers of wealth, how much more should we who live in a highly affluent culture take seriously the economic question."[4] For most of us in our culture, a life of simplicity doesn't come naturally.

PERSONAL RESPONSE Considering what you've learned in the last two days on the discipline of simplicity, what practical steps can you take to pare back in a certain area of your life? Describe.

I hope you've enjoyed these two days as much as I have. After walking through seasons of an overly complicated and at times frenzied life, I love reflecting on what really matters and then arranging my life around those things. The rest of this session, we'll discover that the spiritual discipline of simplicity naturally leads us into the disciplines of generosity and rest. I can't wait to continue the journey with you.

DAY 3

GENEROSITY

Freedom to Give

The cautious faith that never saws off the limb on which it is sitting never learns that unattached limbs may find strange, unaccountable ways of not falling.[5]

—— DALLAS WILLARD

As I've mentioned, and I'm sure you've gathered, the spiritual disciplines often flow in and out of each other so seamlessly that it's hard to know when one ends and the other begins. So today, instead of turning onto Generosity Boulevard from Simplicity Lane, the road we're traveling on is merely about to change names. That's one of the beauties of the spiritual disciplines—they all lead toward the common destination of deepening our relationship with God.

Consider how interconnected simplicity is with generosity. It's impossible to live a generous life while a slave to our money and possessions. We can't give our time if every minute is booked with activity. But when our lives are arranged around the things that matter to the heart of God and we've anchored our hope and trust in Him and not in our stuff, we'll be in position to give generously. And we'll find joy in the process.

You may be wondering why generosity is considered a discipline. Isn't it more a condition of our hearts? Well, yes. But we have to practice the discipline of generosity so our hearts can get into generous shape. Once our giving muscles are toned and our generous reflexes are sharpened, we'll fall in love with experiencing the backward reality Jesus spoke of—it's better to give than to receive (Acts 20:35).

> **PERSONAL REFLECTION** What keeps you from giving generously? Think specifically. It could be anything from a love of possessions to fear of not having enough in savings. We all have different obstacles.

Go back to 1 Timothy 6:17-19 from yesterday's study.

What are the benefits of being rich in good works, generous, and willing to share?

PERSONAL TAKE Paul said that living generously and sacrificially is the way we take hold of the life that is truly life. Why do you think this is so? Take all of verse 19 into consideration.

Read Matthew 6:19-21.

What simple reasons did Jesus give for storing up treasures in heaven and not storing up treasures on earth?

According to verse 21, how do we know where our heart resides?

Read verses 22-23.

The metaphor in verses 22-23 has always been a tricky one for modern-day readers because it's based on an ancient cultural illustration. Think of the eye as a window that separates the inside from the outside of a person. Whatever light the eye perceives illuminates the whole body, but if the eye doesn't perceive light, then the whole body is in darkness. I learned this as a kid while blindfolded and playing Pin the Tail on the Donkey. When my eyes were darkened, so was my whole body. (I feel like this just really dated me.)

Okay, but that still leaves us with a lot of questions about the metaphor. What does an eye have to do with storing up treasures in heaven instead of on earth? It helps immensely to know that the word *healthy* ("eye is healthy") can mean *whole person generosity*, and the word *bad* ("eye is bad") can mean *evil* and *greedy*.[6]

A translation from Jonathan Pennington's book *The Sermon on the Mount and Human Flourishing* helps pull this together.

> The eye is the lamp of the body.
> Therefore, if your eye is whole and
> generous then your whole body will be
> enlightened. But if your eye is evil and
> greedy then your whole body will be
> darkened. Thus, if the light that is in
> you is darkness, what darkness that is![7]
> (vv. 22-23)

How does living generously affect all the other parts of your life? In other words, how does this way of life illuminate every other area?

Conversely, how does being greedy and only looking out for yourself cast darkness on the other parts of your life? Take some time to think about this.

Finish this section by reading verse 24. Your translation may say, "You cannot serve God and mammon" (NKJV). (*Mammon* is a Semitic word for money or possessions.)[8]

Generally speaking, why is it impossible to serve two masters?

Later in the Sermon on the Mount, Jesus explained how our heavenly Father longs to give generously and honestly to us (Matt. 7:9-11). He doesn't deceive or withhold from His children. I get excited about passages that talk about the Lord's ample supply. They reveal that God doesn't need our money or our time, for He is never short on either. We're to cultivate generous hearts and lifestyles because it's in this upside-down way of living where we discover the unexpected delight of helping others and the freedom of entrusting our well-being to our heavenly Father who dresses the lily and nourishes the sparrow.

To quote Dallas Willard once again, "Our need to give is greater than God's need to receive, because he is always well supplied."[9] I love Dallas so much I can hardly stand it. What a brilliant insight.

You've done some soul-searching work this session. I'm proud of you! Simplicity and generosity are counter-cultural ways of living, to be sure, yet they're the ways of Christ. I look forward to ending our session with another against-the-grain spiritual practice, Sabbath rest. At least this is one I think we can all more naturally agree we want and need more of.

Celebrating Redemption

Sabbath is a workshop for
the practice of eternity.[10]

EUGENE PETERSON

Resting, worship, and observing the Sabbath are all interconnected disciplines. We could have easily placed the topic of Sabbath rest in Session Four, which focused on worship, thanksgiving, and celebration. But since the regular rhythm of stopping and resting is so adverse to our culture's interminable drumbeat, placing Sabbath rest in close proximity to solitude and simplicity felt like a nice spot. Plus, these quieter and more introspective disciplines require us to develop many of the same spiritual muscles.

In his book, *Christ Plays in Ten Thousand Places,* Eugene Peterson said this about Sabbath: "The Hebrew word *shabbat,* which we take over into our language untranslated, simply means, 'Quit . . . Stop . . . Take a break.'"[11] While this practice of stopping was a part of normal routine in many societies over the years, the idea is nearly foreign to us. And frankly, it is enormously challenging when productivity and go-go-go are the messages of the day.

The closest most of us come to taking a Sabbath is flying out the door to church on a Sunday morning, scrambling for our seats during the opening song, then frantically maneuvering out of the parking lot after the service to get back home to the casserole in the oven or to a restaurant to beat the brunch crowd. An afternoon soccer or baseball game later, and we find suppertime and bedtime are upon us with all the soon-to-be Monday morning emails and to-do's accumulating before we even hit our pillows. With no heaps of guilt, I don't think this is the Sabbath rest Moses helped establish, nor is it the one Jesus advocated for.

I try hard not to do Monday-through-Friday type work on Sundays, but I'm often guilty of committing the day to other kinds of work. Or I spend all day (post-church) entertaining myself in ways that have little or nothing to do with being in God's presence. While I may feel justified that I'm not doing "work-work" in either of these scenarios, I still fall short of the purpose of Sabbath. Merely refraining from my normal work isn't the ultimate goal; rather it's the means that allows me to worship and enjoy the God of the Sabbath. How easy it is to miss the point of rest when we make the Sabbath about not doing work instead of about *why* we're not supposed to be doing work—to enjoy God.

So today we'll look at the origins of the Sabbath in the Old Testament, and tomorrow we'll follow Jesus through grain fields on the Sabbath and witness Him work Sabbath healings. (Keep in mind that in Jewish culture the Sabbath is observed on Saturday, the seventh day of the week. Most Christians celebrate it on Sunday, the first day of the week.) My prayer is that after these two days of study our understanding of God's heart behind the Sabbath will inspire us to incorporate the spiritual discipline of Sabbath rest into the regular rhythm of our week. And if you're already incorporating an observance of the day, I pray its purpose will come into clearer focus so you can more purposefully protect it and more fully celebrate it.

PERSONAL REFLECTION What has the idea of Sabbath meant to you over the years? How have you observed it? Do you think you sometimes miss the point of Sabbath? If so, how?

Read Exodus 20:1-17.

The Lord told the people of Israel to remember the Sabbath and to keep it _____.

In what ways were the people to accomplish this command?

PERSONAL REFLECTION What is the hardest part about "stopping" for you?

How did God Himself participate in observing a day of rest (v. 11)?

What two actions did God take in relation to the Sabbath? (Circle the correct answers.)

Honored it   Blessed it   Declared it holy   Made it religious

The Hebrew word for *holy* in this passage means *to be set apart.*[12] It can also mean to withdraw "someone or something from profane or ordinary use."[13] It further means *to consecrate*, which is to dedicate something to a particular purpose. In other words, the Sabbath day was to be set apart from the other six days of the week. And it was to be set apart to God.

> **PERSONAL TAKE** In light of these definitions and Exodus 20:8-11, the Israelites were to observe the Sabbath for what purposes?

Read Exodus 31:13-17.

The Sabbath would serve as a sign between God and the Israelites (vv. 13,17). What was the purpose of that sign?

After God gave the Ten Commandments to Israel (Ex. 20), many years and events transpired before He formally reiterated those commands to a subsequent generation. After years of wandering in the wilderness, Israel stood poised to cross the Jordan into the promised land. The essence of God's laws had not changed, but a few laws took on additional shades of meaning, the keeping of the Sabbath being one of them.

Keep a finger or bookmark in Exodus 20 and turn to Deuteronomy 5. Read verses 12-15.

According to verse 15, what significant act had God done for Israel? How does this act tie into God's command for the Israelites to keep the Sabbath?

Compare Exodus 20:11 with Deuteronomy 5:15. How is the reason for keeping the Sabbath in Exodus different from the one given in Deuteronomy?

Sabbath-keeping in the Book of Exodus was rooted in God's creation act in Genesis. Just as God rested from His work on the seventh day after having created the world, so He called His people to rest and celebrate Him and His creation on the Sabbath. But by the time we get to the account in Deuteronomy, Israel had wandered in the wilderness and was about to start anew in the promised land. Now the attention had been turned from Sabbath as creation celebration to Sabbath as redemption celebration.[14] As I write these words, I so badly want to hear an *amen*! We have been created and redeemed by our Savior, and thank God that He graced us with one full day each week to celebrate so great a salvation.

God's deliverance of the Israelites out of Egypt hits close to home for me. He's redeemed me not only for the life to come, but also from my life that was—seasons where I was a slave to myself, without hope. I often remember on Sunday mornings (the day of the week I observe a Sabbath) in my church service how the Lord brought me out of places of darkness with His "strong hand" and "outstretched arm" like He did the people of Israel from the bondage of Egypt.

> PERSONAL REFLECTION How does remembering God's redemption of you further encourage you to set aside the Sabbath and cease from your normal work? Be specific.

Though observing a true Sabbath will indeed renew and refresh us and give us much needed rest, as Eugene Peterson reminded us, "Sabbath is not primarily about us or how it benefits us; it is about God and how God forms us."[15] In our selfie culture where just about everything is meant to be all about us, what a privilege to resist such a small and unsatisfying preoccupation by worshiping our Redeemer.

We'll close our day by reading the only psalm in the psalter specifically designated for the Sabbath. Derek Kidner said this about this psalm, "This Song for the Sabbath is proof enough . . . that the Old Testament sabbath was a day not only for rest but for corporate worship."[16]

Read Psalm 92:1-15.

> PERSONAL TAKE How does this psalm speak to the importance and benefits of weekly Sabbath worship?

These two ideas of rest and corporate worship come together for me on Sunday mornings. It is often the best day of my week for all the fellowship, support, prayer, celebration, spiritual nourishment, seeing some of my favorite children, and simply being together with other believers. I'm not saying I've never been dragged to church, or haven't dragged myself there on occasion, but for the most part I want to be with my local church on Sundays.

Recently I heard a young woman ask the question, "Is it a sin to not go to church?" The only thing I could think was, *This is not the right question!* The better question is, *Why would you ever want to miss the vibrancy of corporate worship on the Sabbath?* I had not an ounce of judgment toward her, only a desire for her to see that trying to get church attendance off the "sin list" is to miss the goodness of Sabbath and the beauty of God as both Creator and Redeemer. I deeply hope you're enjoying the discipline of Sabbath rest and corporate worship in your life.

We'll talk more about rest and Sabbath tomorrow, in particular from a New Testament perspective. In the meantime, I hope you'll reflect on the ancient command and necessity of observing a weekly Sabbath. As we've seen today, if we merely think of it as a day to cease working Monday through Friday yet frantically moving from activity to activity or even lazily flipping from channel to channel, we will miss its divine and glorious purpose. We will miss the celebration of who God is and what He has done for us.

PERSONAL REFLECTION What's one new truth you've learned about Sabbath today? How does it compel you to observe the Sabbath more fully?

The Sabbath Is for Us

> [Sabbath is] a way of working from rest, not for rest, with nothing to prove. A way of bearing fruit from abiding, not ambition.[17]

JOHN MARK COMER

As New Testament believers, we can easily talk ourselves into the idea that the Sabbath is an Old Testament concept to which we're no longer beholden. *Cue the activity*, we think, because now the Sabbath is back on the table as one more free day in our week because, well, you know . . . the New Testament. This is a misguided conclusion, but I admit we arrive here honestly.

By the time we get to the Sabbath as written about in the Gospels, the Jews of Jesus' day had turned the whole glorious observance into a religious burden meant to oppress rather than liberate. We humans can choke the life out of just about any God-given gift; I don't know how we got to be such experts at this. At any rate, this distorting the essence of the Sabbath caused Jesus to react quite strongly to those abusing it. Though He challenged the religiosity of Sabbath observance, He didn't discard the Sabbath nor did He undermine its value. He actually showed us its fullest and truest meaning.

If observing the Sabbath shifted emphasis from Exodus to Deuteronomy, you can imagine the shift that transpired when Jesus revealed His authority over the Sabbath in the New Testament. In many ways the essence of the Sabbath remained the same, but in other ways it was transformed into something brand new. I look forward to following Jesus with you through a few of His most memorable Sabbaths to further discover the Sabbath's ultimate meaning.

Read Matthew 12:1-8.

Why did the Pharisees accuse Jesus and His disciples of breaking the Sabbath?

PERSONAL TAKE Based on Exodus 20:10 and Deuteronomy 5:14, how do you see the Pharisees adding to God's law and making it more burdensome?

The Pharisees were notorious for wanting to adhere to the law of God—not a bad goal in life. The problem is that in trying to keep the law, they created numerous additional ones that only loaded people up with burdensome rules to keep that God never intended. They forbade picking grain and eating it on the Sabbath because they determined that even reaping, winnowing, or threshing grain to prepare a meal went against God's law.[18] Of course, this was only the religious leaders' interpretation of the law. Instead of refuting the Pharisees by arguing they had gone beyond the law, Jesus turned to two stories in the Old Testament to make His point.

> **He referenced the first story in Matthew 12:3-4. What did David do in the house of God that was only lawful for the priests? (You can find the original account in 1 Sam. 21:1-6.)**

Jesus refuted the Pharisees' accusation by referring to a nearly starving David eating consecrated bread in the house of God that was reserved for the priests. His point? If David was justified in eating the bread that symbolized the Presence of God, how much more so were the disciples eating grain on the Sabbath while walking in the actual Presence of God, Jesus Christ Himself?

> **The second Old Testament reference that Jesus made is found in Matthew 12:5. What did the priests do in the temple, yet they were still innocent? (You can find the answer in Numbers 28:9-10.)**

> **In Matthew 12:6, Jesus directly inferred that He is greater than the**
> **_____ .**

> **Even more directly, Jesus claimed in verse 8 that the Son of Man is**
> **_____ of the Sabbath.**

If the priests could make sacrifices in the temple on the Sabbath and be innocent, how much more so were Jesus' disciples innocent when One greater than the temple was among them? When the Lord of the Sabbath was in their midst!

Craig Blomberg succinctly put it this way, "Jesus' sovereign authority will determine how the Sabbath is now fulfilled in the kingdom age."[19] As modern-day believers, we can't fully grasp the significance of Sabbath observance or the centrality of the temple for the Jewish people. They were symbols of national pride. So Jesus' claims would have been staggering for the first-century Pharisee. He was putting Himself above King David and above the Sabbath, two central symbols of Jewish identity.

> PERSONAL REFLECTION How does Jesus being Lord of the Sabbath shape the way you approach this day of the week?

Mark's Gospel records this same story with a slightly different perspective.

Hold your place in Matthew and read Mark 2:23-28.

What important truth did Jesus declare in verse 27 that is not found in Matthew's account?

Only in Mark's Gospel is Jesus quoted as saying the Sabbath is made for men and women, not men and women for the Sabbath. The Pharisees had gotten this turned around, and, as a result, missed the Sabbath's purpose. They saw it as a way to earn their standing before God and others instead of receiving it as a gift that allowed them to enjoy God more fully. The Pharisees had strayed so far from the Sabbath's original design that they preferred Jesus' disciples go hungry on the Sabbath rather than enjoy its benefits. They had made it a restrictive burden, rather than a freeing blessing. Do you ever approach attending church and observing the Sabbath as something you "have to do for God?" If so, think about Jesus' statement that the Sabbath is made for us!

> PERSONAL REFLECTION How does the reality that the Sabbath was made for us reframe the way you think about church and Sabbath rest? In other words, how do you see the Sabbath as something we need rather than something God needs us to take part in?

The Sabbath was first and foremost about enjoying and worshiping God, which is why harvest work had traditionally been set aside. But if you're a disciple following the God of the universe on the Sabbath through stalks of grain, communing with Him, being nourished with every kernel He provides, you better believe you're experiencing to the furthest edges of the field all that the Sabbath was ever meant to be. The Pharisees had missed the true purpose of the Sabbath because they'd missed the One who was in their midst, Jesus as the Son of God.

Before we close, I want to explore one more important aspect of the Sabbath that Jesus went out of His way to highlight.

Turn back to Matthew 12:6-8. Here, Jesus quoted an Old Testament passage from Hosea 6:6.

Fill in the blank: God desires _____ over _____.

How did Jesus use this truth to defend His disciples' actions that day?

It's important that we rid religiosity or legalism from our Sabbath practices. Yes, sometimes we'll go to church when we don't feel like it because we know it's the right thing to do. Or we'll close our computers on the Sabbath because we're disciplining ourselves to do so. But we need always keep in mind that God's compassion, heart, and goodness are at the center of this day. The Sabbath is not about checking off a religious box; it's about setting aside a day of the week to reflect on His words, worship Him, and rest.

Let's see how Jesus' statement about mercy over sacrifice plays out in real life. Read Matthew 12:9-14 and Mark 3:1-6.

What else do you discover about the Sabbath and the heart of God from this story?

From today's passages we've learned that (1) Jesus is Lord of the Sabbath; (2) the Sabbath was created for our benefit; (3) keeping the Sabbath is not about legalism but enjoyment of Jesus; (4) showing compassion on the Sabbath (if a situation arises) is more important to Him than ritual sacrifice.

PERSONAL TAKE How do these scriptural truths expand your view of an ideal Sabbath day for you? How might they limit it? Give this some thought.

PERSONAL REFLECTION Based on what you've learned the past two days, what specific changes do you need to make to protect your Sabbath day so you can worship God, enjoy Him, fully rest both in body and spirit, or even serve someone in need if the opportunity arises? Journal below.

God told the Israelites that the Sabbath would serve as a sign to them throughout the generations, one that would cause them to know that He had set them apart in holiness. Even today, as we observe the Sabbath, we actively remember that God has made us holy and set us apart for His good purposes through His Son Jesus Christ. "Sabbath is a deliberate act of interference, an interruption of our work each week, a decree of no-work so that we are able to notice, to attend, to listen, to assimilate this comprehensive and majestic work of God, to orient our work in the work of God."[20]

Simplicity, Generosity, and Rest

SIMPLICITY

Practicing the discipline of simplicity can be challenging at first, but in the long run it's freeing and rewarding. I'm hesitant to give a how-to on this one because this process can easily become legalistic. But here are some tips on how to get started:

HOW TO SIMPLIFY

- If you're married, and if you have a family, talk to your spouse and children about simplifying not only your possessions but also your time (not running to a million activities in countless directions). If you're single, talk this through with your closest friends.

- Think of areas where you have excess. It may be your wardrobe, pantry, spare bedroom, basement, the amount of cars in your garage, and so forth. (It may surprise you how much stuff you have accumulated.) What can you give away to someone who might need or want what you have?

- Declutter. Get rid of stuff you don't really need. How to choose? The time test—If you haven't used it in months, it might be time to get rid of it. For my birthday a few years ago, I was given my favorite dinnerware line. My sister in-law immediately started packing up my old, but still in great shape, dishes. I wanted to keep both sets. She rightly and wisely wanted to know why. I had no good answer. She's always encouraging me to only keep what I'm using.

- There's also the helpful versus cumbersome test. Ask, *Is this something that is useful to my spiritual life and living in the kingdom, or is it something that is dragging my attention away from the Lord and His purposes?* Obviously not every item in our lives screams "kingdom of God," except maybe our coffee makers. The big idea is to make sure that we're not being drawn away by material possessions or loaded down by excess. We want to live simply so we can live freely.

- Ask and answer this question: *Can I live on less?* If so, sell it, give it away, donate it—whatever you do, simplify.

- Consider your spending habits with your spouse or a close friend(s). There are lots of wonderful resources that can help us be better stewards of our finances. If you choose a book to help you, invite the Lord into the process and let the Holy Spirit lead you.

GENEROSITY

Throughout Scripture, the teaching is clear: we're to be givers. The Old Testament speaks of us giving a tithe, which is ten percent of our income. The New Testament doesn't use that word (or specific amount) but does call us to be "cheerful" givers (2 Cor. 9:7). The Greek word for *cheerful* is *hilaros*, from which we get our word *hilarious*.[21] So we are to be "hilarious" givers—giving joyfully and generously.

The New Testament also speaks of us giving sacrificially, using the example of the Macedonian church who gave willingly, abundantly, and joyfully out of their "extreme poverty" (2 Cor. 8:1-5).

Keep in mind:

- God owns everything. Each of us are stewards of all He's given us.

- View generosity as a lifestyle, not as a one-time activity. Make it a way of life.

- If you're not currently giving, make a decision to give on a regular basis. Pray about what you should give and be consistent.

- Decide on a percentage you can give to your local church or a Christ-centered ministry and follow through. Or decide on a fixed amount you want to give but revisit that amount every few months if you feel it's not enough. If you're a business owner or self-employed, you may want to designate a certain part of your business as an income stream you give away. If your income fluctuates, on top of your regular giving, you may give extra if you hit a certain sales number or if your bonus is over a certain amount.

The point is not to get legalistic with this. Nor is it to try to earn favor with God. Giving is a blessing and a way of tangibly participating in God's kingdom. It's not about giving away ten percent and keeping ninety percent for ourselves. It's all God's. Be creative. Be lavish. And ask the Lord to show you the blessings of living generously.

REST

Finding time for Sabbath may be difficult, but it is more needed than we think. In a culture that prizes later and longer workdays and extremely hectic weekends, we need to be proactive about taking a weekly Sabbath. How can you build this time into your life?

- Be intentional. If you don't block a day a week that's free from extraneous activities, it probably won't happen.

- If it's possible, choose your Sabbath to be on the day you worship corporately at church. For most of us, this is on Sunday, though some have unique situations that may allow for being in church on Sunday without allowing time for a Sabbath until Wednesday or Saturday.

- Understand the Sabbath's purpose. Use it for rest, refreshing, and worship. What activities provide this for you? It has been said that if you work with your mind, Sabbath with your hands. If you work with your hands, Sabbath with your mind.[22] This has been very helpful for me.

- Your Sabbath can be filled with the same restful schedule each week, or you can change up how you spend it. Don't be a slave to a certain agenda. Just make sure you set aside that one day a week to enjoy time with the Lord, enjoy others, and lay down the regular tools of work.

WATCH SESSION SIX VIDEO

DISCUSSION QUESTIONS

What's something that really stood out to you in the video teaching?

How have you experienced the pressure to run harder and accumulate more? How has that affected your spiritual life?

What does it mean to store up treasures in heaven? Which would you say you've been more concerned about—storing up treasures in heaven or on earth? Explain.

Jesus taught about God's care for the birds of the air and flowers of the field. Which illustration resonated with you the most, and why?

Jesus said where are our treasure is, there our hearts will be also. What does that mean and how have you seen your heart follow your treasure?

What does it mean to live generously? What are the characteristics of a person who lives generously? Would you describe yourself in that way? Why or why not?

How is living generously about more than just the way you handle money?

Has God ever asked you to leave your "gold" for "the boot"? Share what God taught you through that process.

What does it mean to live simply so we can live ready? How well are you doing that? Explain.

SESSION SEVEN

Engage

JOURNALING THE SESSION

Use this page throughout your session of study. We've given you some prompts, but feel free to write other thoughts and questions to help you learn and process the spiritual disciplines of fellowship, confession, submission, and service.

PREPARING FOR THE SESSION

Before you start your work this session, journal some of your thoughts about the disciplines of fellowship, confession, submission, and service. How have you practiced these disciplines in the past? What has hindered your practice of these disciplines? What do you hope to get out of this session?

DURING THE SESSION

What are some key things you're learning this session about the disciplines of fellowship, confession, submission, and service?

REVIEWING THE SESSION

What are your biggest takeaways from this session, and how will you put them into practice?

Session Seven Introduction

As we begin our final session of *Encountering God*, we're pulling away from the countryside of simplicity, generosity, and rest and are about to enter the bustling town square of fellowship, serving, and togetherness. One thing is certain about the Christian faith—it is not a private religion. It's meant to be lived out in the context of community.

I must say, writing about these more corporate and relational disciplines has proven tricky. It's no longer just us in the woods with our Bibles. Or on a prayer walk with our favorite travel mugs of tea. People complicate the spiritual disciplines. I complicate them. You start adding people to the mix, and you get lots of opinions, personalities, hairstyles, different ways of doing things, and so on. Yet it is within our social contexts where we engage the outward disciplines and where iron sharpens iron. This means we get to put our quieter times with the Lord into action by loving our neighbors through serving, staying accountable to one another, and being intentional about fellowshipping with other believers. These outward disciplines not only counterbalance the inward ones, they fuel one another.

My hope is that in this session you and I will have a renewed vision of the outward and relational disciplines of fellowship, service, confession, and submission. We'll look at the spirit and purpose of each of them. How we engage in these disciplines might look different across different settings and in different churches, but engaging in them is what's important. And make no mistake, all the treasures we've gained on those quieter, earlier stretches of road with the Lord are stowed in our hearts and will flow out of us in community. They'll make all the difference as we engage in these outward disciplines.

In *Lord, Teach Us: The Lord's Prayer and the Christian Life,* William H. Willimon and Stanley Hauerwas wrote, "Christianity is inherently communal, a matter of life in the Body, the church. Jesus did not call isolated individuals to follow him. He called a group of disciples."[1] This excites me. Not only do we not have to go through life alone, we're not even supposed to! As much as some of us may thrive in quieter settings, the treasures gained there would mean little if not for the fellowship, serving, hospitality, accountability, and sheer friendship of the body of Christ. As Reuben Welch succinctly put it, "We really do need each other."[2]

Yet it is precisely this rich, communal living within the body of Christ that I fear is waning. Our Western society tends to prize individualism and individual contributions over family and groups. As a generalization, we like the idea of independence, which can spill over into our spiritual lives. Even for those who see the importance of belonging to the fellowship of believers, we sometimes "outgrow" these communal disciplines in the name of "Christian freedom." Isn't there grace if we don't want to serve? Do we really have to do all this?

But Paul told us we're to strengthen one another's faith (Rom. 1:12), carry one another's burdens (Gal. 6:2), be kind to one another (Eph. 4:32), and build each other up (1 Thes. 5:11). James said we're to pray for one another (Jas. 5:16). The author of Hebrews encouraged us to not neglect gathering together (Heb. 10:25). Jesus said we're to wash one

> One thing is certain about the Christian faith—it is not a private religion. It's meant to be lived out in the context of community.

another's feet (John 13:14). All these references just scratch the surface. So, yes, we do need to be committed to fellowship, but hopefully this will be more of a joyful experience than a dutiful discipline.

Dallas Willard wrote, "Not every act that *may* be done as a discipline *need* be done as a discipline."[3] This is an especially applicable insight for Session Seven. A lot of the disciplines we'll look at this session won't necessarily feel like spiritual disciplines. Many will spring from our hearts as part of life's rhythms. We'll want to do them because we love the people around us. For instance, if I have a cold and you serve me by dropping chicken soup off at my doorstep, you probably won't sign your note, "I really had to discipline myself to do this. Love, your dear friend." So what you might find this session is that you're already practicing a bunch of disciplines you didn't even know were disciplines.

My hope and prayer is that after this session you'll be convinced of how essential you are to your community of faith. And how essential that community is to you. Oh, and I should mention, this is not the session where introverts get to claim a pass. My extrovert friends have already been complaining to me about all this reflection and solitude and simplicity we've been having. So welcome to this week's party. We're all in this together.

A Place of Belonging

We belong to one another only through and in Jesus Christ.[4]

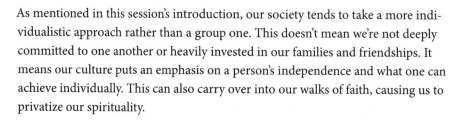

DIETRICH BONHOEFFER

As mentioned in this session's introduction, our society tends to take a more individualistic approach rather than a group one. This doesn't mean we're not deeply committed to one another or heavily invested in our families and friendships. It means our culture puts an emphasis on a person's independence and what one can achieve individually. This can also carry over into our walks of faith, causing us to privatize our spirituality.

First-century Jews were all about the family. Scholar Craig Blomberg stated: "The ancient Mediterranean personality was far more group-centered than we are with our rugged, Western individualism."[5] This understanding will give us an even greater insight into the beauty and power of New Testament fellowship as we look at this gift (and "discipline") in today's study.

Read Matthew 12:46-49. In a setting of tight-knit families, we see Jesus broke through with a profound teaching.

> Who did Jesus define as His family over and above His physical family?

If this feels off-putting to us as modern-day readers, we can only imagine how Jesus' statements landed in a culture wholly bound to kin. The flipside of this announcement is the inbreaking of an extraordinary new family where every person is welcome! Wealthy, healthy, sick, poor, elite, broken, bruised, powerful—all make up the body of Christ, His church. This session we'll see how our spiritual family is to sacrifice for, serve, encourage, support, pray for, and love one another. We're also to carry one another's burdens. When the church loves like Christ, there's nothing in the world like her.

PERSONAL REFLECTION Have other believers cared for you in a way that was as deep or even deeper than care you received from flesh and blood family members? If so, describe what this meant to you.

Sacrificial love shared within the church is Christ's ideal. But some of the ways Christians have treated one another throughout our history has been scandalous by His standards. We must honestly admit that Christ's body doesn't always act like the loving family it's supposed to. Part of my hope for this session's study is that you and I will gain a renewed sense of what it means to be part of the fellowship of believers, deepening our commitment to one another and to Christ our Brother.

Let's explore the New Testament idea of fellowship. The Greek word used for *fellowship* is *koinonia*, which might be familiar to you. It means *fellow* and *participant* and implies fellowship or sharing with someone or in something.[6] In the New Testament, it means to share in the life of Christ and in the lives of one another through the bond of Christ. We can cherish, love, and share friendship with those who are not followers of Jesus, but we won't have fellowship with them as defined in the New Testament. Fellowship is unique to believers because it centers on the shared life of Christ and is fueled by the Holy Spirit.

Shortly after Christ's ascension, the nature of the community of God's people changed forever. Let's briefly look at the events surrounding the birth of the church.

Read Acts 1:4-8; 2:1-4.

What would God's people receive with the coming of the Holy Spirit (1:8)?

The people were _____ with the Holy Spirit (2:4).

Read Acts 2:32-33,38-39.

How did Luke describe the way the Holy Spirit came in verse 33?

Luke said in verse 38 that Peter told the crowd that if they repented and were baptized, they would receive the _____ of the Holy Spirit.

> **PERSONAL TAKE** The Holy Spirit ignited the inauguration of the church. Do you see today's church relying on Him as the essence of the fellowship of believers? Explain your thoughts.

Let's read on to see the practical outflow of the Holy Spirit's presence in the church community. I love this! Read Acts 2:42-47.

What four things did the early church devote themselves to as a result of the Holy Spirit's coming (v. 42)?

1.

2.

3.

4.

Circle number two since it's today's focus.

Using five adjectives, describe the community according to verses 46-47. (These are your own adjectives based on the picture painted in the text.)

Remember, these passages are descriptive, not prescriptive. They describe how the early church responded to the Holy Spirit rather than prescribe exactly how we're to respond today. I don't think any of us are in the habit of going to the temple daily or hopping from house to house for dinner. But regular fellowship should look like something in our lives. The whole of the New Testament assumes it. Committing to fellowship may begin as a discipline, but hopefully it will weave itself into the rhythms and fabric of our routines. *Koinonia* can be planned, but it will also happen spontaneously in our homes, when we run into a friend in the grocery store, or linger in conversation on the phone.

Read Hebrews 10:24-25.

What did the author of Hebrews caution us to not neglect doing?

Verse 25 says that some are in the _____ of not gathering together.

We all have reasons why we get out of the habit of consistent fellowship. We're busy, working two jobs, in grad school, remodeling our homes, exhausted, have four kids playing sports. We find the people at our office who don't claim to be Christ-followers easier to get along with and possibly more fun. We're afraid if we join a Bible study we won't know enough or be judged. We'd rather sleep in on Sundays because it's the only day out of the week we can actually catch our breaths. What have I left out?

I appreciate this passage in Hebrews because apparently committing to fellowship isn't a new challenge. At the very beginning of the church's history, people were prone to fall out of the habit of gathering together. At the same time, note the characteristics of what the early church gathering was supposed to look and feel like.

According to verses 24-25, describe the characteristics of the gathering. What are we supposed to do for each other?

Something that's unique about Christian fellowship is that we can't have fellowship with each other if we don't first have it with Jesus. And if we have fellowship with Jesus, we will long for it with others. Let me show you what I mean.

Read 1 Corinthians 1:4-9.

In verse 9, Paul said we were called into _____ with whom?

Read Philippians 3:8-10.

Whose sufferings are we to fellowship in?

We're to have our own fellowship with the Lord. There's no substitute for our personal communion with Him. We'll close by looking at how John blended personal fellowship with God and fellowship with each other.

Read 1 John 1:1-4.

Whom did John have fellowship with (v. 3)?

John made known to his readers what he had personally experienced while walking with Jesus—what he'd heard from Him, what he'd seen from Him. John did this for what purpose (v. 3)?

> **PERSONAL TAKE** John gave us a lot to think about here. Why do we have to have fellowship with Christ in order to have it with other believers? And why does our fellowship with Christ make us want to share in fellowship with other believers?

What did all of this fellowship culminate in (v. 4)? (Circle the correct answer.)

Duty   Discipline   Joy   Thanks

When I wrote *What Love Is*, a Bible study on 1, 2, & 3 John, what struck me over and over was John's palpable passion for the fellowship of believers. When you read the opening lines of 1 John, you can almost feel John reaching through the pages to us with outstretched arms.

He had personally experienced being in relationship with Jesus and with the disciples, and now he wanted his readers to experience the joy of being in that same kind of fellowship.

PERSONAL PRAYER If you're out of the habit of fellowship, take a moment to go to the Holy Spirit with whatever is keeping you from a community of believers.

As we close today's study on fellowship, my heart for the church is renewed. I'm stirred by the power of the Holy Spirit in our midst, the joy this perpetuates, the love and care we're to have for one another, the anchor of belonging to a family where Christ is our brother.

PERSONAL TAKE Why do you think church history has often included fellowship as one of the spiritual disciplines?

PERSONAL REFLECTION What has encouraged you or challenged you the most about today's study on fellowship, and why?

The rest of this session we'll continue to look at some of the practical expressions of being part of God's family. But for today, I'll leave you with Paul's final words in his second letter to the Corinthians:

Finally, brothers and sisters, rejoice.
Become mature, be encouraged, be of
the same mind, be at peace, and the
God of love and peace will be with you.
Greet one another with a holy kiss. All
the saints send you greetings. The grace
of the Lord Jesus Christ, and the love
of God, and the fellowship of the Holy
Spirit be with you all.
2 CORINTHIANS 13:11-13

Releasing Our Burdens

He who is alone with his sin is utterly alone.[7]

DIETRICH BONHOEFFER

When my nephew Will was eight, he went through a little mischievous phase. I am his adoring aunt, so I classify this season as "experiential development." (Incidentally, his parents classify it as something far less endearing.) He was getting into all sorts of things he wasn't supposed to, much of which was mildly damaging to the house—meaning my sister-in-law Megen was about to give me legal guardianship. The final straw was when Will stained the new bathroom floor with ink from a pen he had been playing with. My brother David tried to get to the bottom of the great ink-pen-disassemblement.

"Will, I don't understand what's happening," he said. "There was the window screen incident, the clogged sink drain, now the pen and the ink on the newly tiled bathroom floor. And there was something else you did recently that I can't remember . . ."

Will pointed toward his chest of drawers. "You forgot about the dresser."

"That's right!" David exclaimed. "There was the drawing you etched into the top of your dresser that we can't get out!"

When David told me this story, we could hardly contain ourselves. It was classic Will to offer up past offenses, even the ones David couldn't remember. He has always been an avid confessor, which I'm convinced will serve him well in life. "You forgot about the dresser" is one of our favorite lines—a perennial reminder of what an honest and open life looks like.

In Session Three, we looked at confession before the Lord. Today we'll focus on confession within the community of believers. Don't be alarmed. Confession to others is a practice unique to the fellowship of believers, and it's actually a gift we probably don't talk about enough. In his book *Life Together*, Dietrich Bonhoeffer framed confession as the blessing it is when he said, ". . . confession is not a law, it is an offer of divine help for the sinner."[8] Out of the deep and swirling waters of guilt and repetitive sin, I have grasped this hand of divine help more times than I can remember. And by God's grace, I have been able to extend that hand to others who needed a person to whom they could confess. This is another gift of being part of the body of Christ.

Read Proverbs 28:13.

How have you found this proverb to be true in your life?

Read James 5:13-16.

What did James instruct us to do in verse 16? What will be the result?

Why do you think James told us to confess our sins to one another instead of solely to God? List all the reasons you can think of.

PERSONAL TAKE How do you see confession and healing as being interrelated?

PERSONAL REFLECTION How does verse 16 encourage you to be intentional about praying for another person's healing? (Always keeping in mind that we're to trust God with the results.)

Read Romans 12:4-5 and Ephesians 4:25.

Paul said we are _____ of one another.

Opening up to others and sharing our burdens typically doesn't come naturally to us. We like to deal with things on our own, privately, internally, thank you very much. Yet Paul said that we belong to one another as members of Christ's family. This means we have the blessing of being able to share with a trusted believer or two what is tempting us, has overtaken us, is causing us unbearable guilt or shame. This can be unsettling, even terrifying, at first. But sharing with trusted people who genuinely love Jesus is one of the most liberating gifts we have as believers. And as James said, it leads to healing.

Read 2 Corinthians 4:1-2.

Why is it necessary to renounce secret and shameful practices?

PERSONAL TAKE How does appropriate confession to trusted people around us keep us from living a life inhabited by secrecy, shame, and deceit?

I love the idea of being able to walk freely before God and others with a clear conscience. I have not always lived in this freedom, so when I read 2 Corinthians 4:1-2, its truth rings of a gift for which I am most grateful—peace.

Read 1 John 1:5-7.

If we walk in the light as He is in the light, we have fellowship with

_____ _____.

This is such a fascinating passage. I logically expect the verse to read that if we walk in the light as Jesus is in the light, we will have fellowship with Jesus. And while this is certainly true, that's not what this verse leads to. Walking in the light with Christ results in rich, open, and deep fellowship with one another. Part of what is so devastating about harboring sin is that it obstructs our relationships with each other. It isolates us. And this is what Satan wants. He wants us cut off from one another, believing we're simply unforgivable or that our brothers and sisters in Christ are so judgmental we could never tell them the truth. But Jesus offers a way of liberation.

Read 1 John 1:8-10; 2:1-2.

What is Jesus faithful to do when we confess our sins to Him (note both responses)?

According to 1:10, what is universally true about all of us?

If we're all sinners, no one should ever treat another sinner judgmentally or with disdain. After all, as Bonhoeffer beautifully said, we all live "under the cross."[9] That should make us safe people to whom anyone could confess his or her sins.

1 John 2:1 says we have an _____ with the Father.

The word *advocate* is unique to John's writings. It means to intercede on *behalf of, help,* or *comfort*.[10] In other words, Jesus is our Advocate before the Father when we sin. This is expounded upon in verse 2.

1 John 2:2 says Jesus is the _____ _____ for our sins.

When Jesus sacrificed his life for us on the cross, He became the atoning sacrifice, or propitiation, for our sins. This phrasing carries the idea of Jesus removing our guilt as well as Him absorbing God's anger toward sinners. The important concept here is that Jesus once and for all took upon Himself the consequences and punishment of our sin. We are all sinners, but through Christ we are also all forgiven. We need to remind each other of this as we walk through life together.

Bonhoeffer said, "In confession occurs the break-through to the Cross."[11] Once again, he made the argument that the reason we find it so difficult to confess our sin or admit our struggles is because it hurts our pride. But this is exactly what needs to happen because our pride is innately set against the work of Jesus on the cross. When we confess to others, the issues we're dealing with or the sins we've committed, we're confessing that we need Jesus as our Advocate, as our atoning sacrifice. And when the person we confess to is a humble believer who also realizes his or her need for Jesus, we won't be judged or beaten down, but rather loved and restored.

In closing today, I want you to be encouraged by one of my favorite passages in Galatians.

Read Galatians 6:1-3.

With what kind of spirit are we to restore someone who has confessed sin to us? What kind of specific actions might that spirit translate into?

What are we to watch out for, and why?

PERSONAL TAKE Think of a time when someone confessed a sin or struggle to you and you helped carry that person's burden. Or think of a time when you confessed a sin or struggle to someone and he/she helped carry your burden. How was your relationship with Christ and that person enriched by the experience?

One of the gifts my parents gave me that I'm most grateful for is a home where confession was encouraged. Confessing my sin and struggles to friends or saying "I'm sorry" when I'm wrong or bringing something in my heart to light because I don't want to live in darkness have been life-saving practices. I simply don't know where I'd be or the toll that harboring sin would have taken on me if I hadn't been taught that confession is literally good for the soul. I have often said that no one person knows all my struggles or each of my sins, but every sin and every struggle is known by someone. I'm thankful for this.

Without a doubt, some of my richest experiences with other believers have taken place when we've been open about our burdens and spoken honestly about the sins, struggles, and doubts we're dealing with. This isn't about oversharing or harping on the past; it's about reminding one another that we have an Advocate, that we're forgiven, and that together we can walk in the light as He is in the light.

> **PERSONAL RESPONSE** Do you have a sin or struggle you need to confess to someone? It can be something you've done or something you're dealing with. Assuming you've already confessed your sin to the Lord, make a commitment to share with a trusted believer. Confession is a gift.

I'll leave you with this insightful quote by Dallas Willard: "We must accept the fact that unconfessed sin is a special kind of burden or obstruction in the psychological as well as the physical realities of the believer's life. The discipline of confession and absolution [forgiveness] removes that burden."[12] May your burden be removed by the work of Jesus and may it be shared by a friend who claims His Name. Amen.

Looking Out for Each Other

The Way of Jesus knows no submission outside the context of *mutual* submission of all to all.[13]

DALLAS WILLARD

Genuine spiritual authority is to be found only where the ministry of hearing, helping, bearing, and proclaiming is carried out.[14]

DIETRICH BONHOEFFER

I'm not sure a word exists in our culture or the church that's more of a lightning rod than the word *submission*. Parents, spouses, and spiritual leaders have at times misused the concept of submission for selfish and manipulative ends—this is not the submission of the New Testament. So perhaps the best place to start is by defining what biblical submission is not. It is not a one-way street where one person calls all the shots. Neither is it to be used to justify abusive relationships, for personal gain, or selfish ends. Submission is not codependency.

For all the misuses, you can imagine why I'm hesitant to write about the spiritual discipline of submission. At the same time, perhaps the distorted meanings are all the more reason to underscore the goodness of what the apostles put forth in the New Testament. They detailed the humility, kindness, trustworthiness, and hospitableness that was necessary for someone to walk in the place of an overseer. To top it off, they presented the idea of mutual submission in their teaching on the subject. No one was ever operating rogue.

Before jumping into Scripture, I have one more thought for consideration. Too often we hear of godly people we know or respected people in ministry going off the rails in some fashion. The details of each story differs, but almost every situation involves lack of accountability. At some point, the guilty party isolates himself or herself, stops taking counsel, and hides his or her behavior. It is actually a lack of healthy submission that so often contributes to distorted versions of it.

So with all this said, I hope to take a fresh look at this somewhat neglected practice and recover the spirit of this discipline. When rightly expressed, submission is one of the most beautiful of the spiritual practices, a discipline that is life-giving, safe-guarding, and guidance-giving. Let's first see how Jesus modeled it.

Read John 6:38.

What did Jesus describe as being His purpose on earth?

Read Luke 22:39-42.

How did Jesus submit His will to the Father's?

PERSONAL TAKE Sometimes we miss that Jesus submitted to the Father during His life on earth. How does Jesus' intimate and healthy submission to the Father differ from the distorted versions we sometimes see?

Read Ephesians 5:15-21.

What exhortation did Paul give the Ephesians in verses 15-16, and why?

What did Paul want them to understand (v. 17)? I love this! We'll come back to it in a moment.

What does being filled with the Holy Spirit look like in Christian fellowship? Describe in your own words the picture given in verses 19-21.

Verse 21 says we're to submit to _____ _____.

Mutual submission is a voluntary yielding to one another in humility. It has to do with putting others before ourselves while also paying attention to their wisdom, insights, cautions, and rebukes. When Paul told us in verse 17 to "understand what the Lord's will is," I'm not sure he was directly connecting that thought to the one of mutual submission in verse 21. But it has sure been my experience that God's will for my life is more fully fleshed out when communing with other believers.

We'll always have a clearer and sounder sense of what His will is when we're committed to seeking it in the context of fellowship.

Receiving guidance is a practice some see as a spiritual discipline in its own right. For the sake of time, I've tucked it in today's study on submission because we often receive guidance by asking for counsel and yielding ourselves to it when appropriate.

Read Proverbs 15:22-23,31-33.

Summarize what these proverbs tell us about seeking counsel.

PERSONAL TAKE How is seeking out and responding to godly counsel a natural part of submission?

In May of my senior year in high school, I lost a basketball scholarship due to injuries on the team I was supposed to be joining—they ended up needing a different position than the one I played. The coach violated NCAA rules by going back on her offer, and my parents could have legally challenged the decision. That late in the year, all the rosters that might have been available to me were full, and I had no place to go. I was devastated. I wanted my parents to fight the decision. Neither of them felt this was the right approach, and they sensed God's hand in the scholarship falling through. We talked and talked; we prayed together, and in the end, I felt that submitting to their counsel was the best and safest decision for me. It was not without pain. I was torn up about the loss well into my college years.

But looking back, I have no regrets. There's no question in my mind my parents were right in spotting God's hand in that pulled scholarship, painful as it was. They were able to see a bigger picture I couldn't see at the time. Submitting to them not only protected me from what might have been, it also led me down a path in music, which led me to Nashville, which oddly enough led me to writing Bible studies.

Let's now look at the idea of submission as it relates to our church leaders. I don't presume to know how this should look in your church, so we'll just look at the spirit and purpose behind submitting to godly leaders.

Read Hebrews 13:17.

What task is a good spiritual leader entrusted with?

The verb *keep watch* means "to be sleepless."[15] The conversation about submission has needed this lovely imagery! We get a shepherdly picture of one who cares so much for those they oversee that they're willing to forgo their own basic needs for what the people they're looking after need. The word also means "to be alertly concerned about."[16] So many of my past and present spiritual leaders, male and female, who resemble this imagery come to mind. This is not to say I haven't had bad experiences with leaders distorting a proper view of submission, but rather to emphasize I've had many good ones.

The author of Hebrews also said that spiritual overseers will one day give an account (to the Lord). How should this motivate spiritual leaders to live in holiness and humility, never abusing their role as overseers?

Read 1 Peter 5:1-5.

Peter juxtaposed three characteristics of an elder in the church (vv. 2-3). Fill in the corresponding pairs below.

THEY ARE NOT TO	THEY ARE TO

PERSONAL TAKE Why do you think it was beneficial for this younger group in the church to submit to their elders? How do you see our culture lacking in this area? (Keep in mind the healthy context in 1 Peter—this exhortation was never about level-headed youth submitting to untrustworthy adults. Also, remember the balance in Scripture—Paul told Timothy not to be ashamed of his youth but to be an example to other believers (1 Tim. 4:12).

Certainly the distortions and abuses surrounding submitting to spiritual authority and to one another have contributed to some hurdles that now lie in the way of this spiritual discipline. We as believers must be vigilant to combat these abuses when they present themselves. But a distortion of something is not a reason to reject the genuine article.

Thinking of submission as a spiritual discipline may seem strange because submitting to someone isn't something you check off your list. It's not an activity per se. Yet I suppose it has found its place on the "spiritual disciplines list" because without it we're untethered, left to our own devices, answering to no one. This is decidedly at odds with what it means to be part of the body of Christ. If this describes you, don't miss the anchoring of a local church, find a godly mentor, and seek the counsel of a wise leader who loves the Lord. You will find it to be less a discipline and more an enriching way of life, full of giving and receiving.

I am daily grateful for the covering that submitting to humble and healthy people provides. Whether it's my pastors, lay-leaders who hold no official title other than that they love the Lord deeply and are committed to my well-being, or my dear friends and family members who regularly love and challenge me, I pray I will always be humbly accountable to godly men and women. And on the occasion where a few may choose to be accountable to me, I pray I will be as one willing to go sleepless on their behalf.

True Greatness

> Not every act of service will, or even should, be disciplined serving. Most of the time our service should spring simply from our love for God and love for others . . . as a result of the life-transforming presence and work of the Holy Spirit.[17]

DONALD WHITNEY

I so appreciate Donald Whitney's sentiment here. Serving others shouldn't be this glum duty where we slump around like a sack of watermelons is strapped to our backs . . . in the name of Jesus. At the same time, sometimes we don't feel like serving. Whitney also wrote, "Two of the deadliest of our sins—sloth and pride—loathe serving."[18]

So there's also that convicting insight.

In my experience, disciplining myself to serve when I didn't feel like it has often resulted in a joy of serving I wasn't expecting. Other times serving remained a challenge that required me to draw on God's strength to accomplish the task. In both cases, I've grown in the process. Whether serving comes naturally or it's something you have to work at, we'll see how fundamental a serving spirit is to the heart of Jesus. And how necessary each of our gifts is to the body of Christ.

Read John 13:12-17.

What did Jesus do for His disciples?

What did Jesus tell His disciples to do, and why (vv. 14-17)?

Jesus said that if His disciples would do these things they would be _____ (v. 17). (Circle the correct answer.)

Rewarded   Exalted   Humbled   Blessed

In the ancient world, hosts offered the common courtesy of washing the feet of their guests. However, the most menial of slaves would typically be the one to carry out the task.[19] But on this occasion, Jesus took up the basin and towel. After all this time of living life with His disciples, Jesus was making a profound point to them.

Most every year at JMI's Jungle Pastor's Conference in the Amazon, we end our session with a foot washing ceremony where we wash the feet of our jungle pastors. It never ceases to be a profoundly moving and emotional experience. It's deeply meaningful because we are tangibly participating in a physical action of Jesus, a sacrament of sorts. But perhaps more meaningful than the act itself is the spirit of humility it requires. Knees on concrete, necks craned downward, thumbs pressed into the feet of gospel-bearers necessitates a heart that has bowed itself to King Jesus. The physical posture of foot washing expresses an inward reality that we are there to serve, and lowering ourselves for others is our joy and privilege.

Since foot washing doesn't appear to have grown into a major practice of the early church, I believe Jesus was modeling a lifestyle of servanthood and humility more than anything else.

Drop down a few verses and read verses 34-35.

How will the world around us know we're Jesus' disciples?

Now read Luke 22:24-27.

What did Jesus teach about who is truly great?

The Jewish culture of Jesus' day was very honor/shame-based, meaning individuals and families did whatever they could to maximize their honor in society and minimize anything that might be shameful. We see Jesus turning these ideals on their head, putting forth a new definition of true greatness—servant leadership.

In what specific ways do you see our current culture (even church culture) at odds with a lifestyle that serves and sacrifices for others? Why do you think we prize our own greatness, comfort, and success over serving others?

Read Mark 10:45. Mark's words reflect the dialogue on servanthood and greatness we just read about in Luke.

How do Jesus' words about His own life and purpose set the precedent for how we're to live ours?

Now that we've looked at the servant heart of Christ, let's look at how the early church lived this out.

Read Galatians 5:13-15.

What is our freedom in Christ supposed to be used for?

PERSONAL TAKE How is all of God's law fulfilled in loving our neighbor as ourselves? In other words, how does this single command essentially fulfill all the others? Keep in mind that Matthew 22:37 says that the greatest command is to love the Lord our God with all our heart, soul, and mind. Yet when we love Him wholly, we will naturally love others as well. So Paul wasn't excluding the command to love God; rather he knew that in order to love others we must first love God.

Read 1 Peter 4:7-11.

What has each person in Christ's body received (v. 10)?

What are we to do with that gift? And how does this make us good stewards of God's grace (v. 10)?

True/False: We're to serve out of the strength God provides, not out of our own reservoirs (v. 11).

What is the ultimate purpose of our serving (v. 11)?

PERSONAL REFLECTION How does this passage excite you about what you personally have to offer to the fellowship of believers?

I love this passage from 1 Peter for so many reasons, but I have to especially appreciate Peter's postscript to showing hospitality in verse 9—"Be hospitable to one another without complaining." What in the world is hospitality if we can't complain a little about what all the people we're being hospitable toward are doing or not doing? Peter's not letting anything slide today.

I want us to close by looking at a passage in 1 Corinthians that further explains the different gifts the Holy Spirit has given to each of us. We'll see with more detail what the practical outpouring of the Spirit looks like in our relationships and communities.

Read 1 Corinthians 12:4-11.

The same Spirit gives many different _____ (v. 4).

True/False: The gifts the Spirit gives us are private and for our personal benefit.

In verse 7, Paul said that a manifestation of the Spirit is given to each person for the common good. I love how Eugene Peterson paraphrased it in The Message: "Each person is given something to do that shows who God is." God has given you something to do, by the power of the Holy Spirit, for the common good of the believers around you, that reflects His character. This is truly incredible.

PERSONAL TAKE How does the reality that God gave you unique gifts to share with Christ's body reframe your idea of serving?

God has given you Spirit-empowered abilities to serve Him and His church. But He has also shaped you to serve the body of Christ through your natural talents, skills, and passions.

PERSONAL REFLECTION What are some of your gifts, passions, or skills you've been called to share with others? How are you sharing them, or how do you plan to share them? Give this some time and thought.

Beyond the church walls, serving can manifest itself as babysitting for neighbors, taking meals to families in flux, running errands for the homebound, providing transportation for the one whose car breaks down, helping with lawn or home maintenance, feeding pets and watering plants for vacationers, and—hardest of all—displaying a servant's heart in the home. Serving typically looks as unspectacular as the practical needs it seeks to meet.[20]

DONALD WHITNEY

We don't have to get fancy or elaborate with serving. We don't have to run out and start a non-profit tomorrow. Remember what Jesus modeled in John 13—humility, love, care, and a servant's heart. This is what He's asking of us.

DAY 5

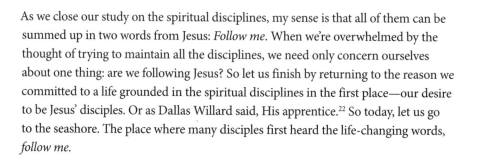

Follow Me

JESUS

If you want to experience the *life* of Jesus, you have to adopt the *lifestyle* of Jesus.[21]

JOHN MARK COMER

As we close our study on the spiritual disciplines, my sense is that all of them can be summed up in two words from Jesus: *Follow me*. When we're overwhelmed by the thought of trying to maintain all the disciplines, we need only concern ourselves about one thing: are we following Jesus? So let us finish by returning to the reason we committed to a life grounded in the spiritual disciplines in the first place—our desire to be Jesus' disciples. Or as Dallas Willard said, His apprentice.[22] So today, let us go to the seashore. The place where many disciples first heard the life-changing words, *follow me*.

Read Matthew 8:18-22.

These verses cover a short account of two would-be followers of Jesus. For the longest time, I glossed over these verses, never paying too much attention to them. That is, until I understood that Matthew strategically placed them here because of something important he wanted us to see.

We'll call the scribe in verse 19 "Disciple A" and the disciple in verse 21 "Disciple B." Fill out the table below.

HIS OFFER TO JESUS	JESUS' RESPONSE
Disciple A	
Disciple B	

We're not told what eventually happened with each of these "disciples," but the impression is that neither ended up following Him, at least not in the moment, the way some of Jesus' disciples had (Matt. 4:18-22). But we'll get to that soon. First, let's look at each "disciple" in turn.

Disciple A was an overeager disciple. He wanted to follow Jesus, but he hadn't yet considered the cost. Earlier in the chapter, Matthew detailed three miracles Jesus had performed. Perhaps this scribe was caught up in the hype, attracted to those miracles and Jesus' powerful authority (Matt. 7:28).

What does Jesus' response to Disciple A tell us about the nature of what it meant to follow Jesus in that moment?

Hold your finger in Matthew and look up Philippians 3:20.

What did Paul tell us about our true home?

Back to Matthew 8. It certainly seems reasonable that the scribe would opt for the familiarity and safety of shore and home over a life of following Jesus. But this is to miss that being with Jesus is our true home. In His presence is our place of security, comfort, and rest. The scribe didn't understand that the comforts and familiarity of a physical home can't compare to the gift of Jesus' presence.

PERSONAL REFLECTION How has Jesus' presence been a place of security and comfort to you? How is He more reliable, more sure than any temporary place on earth?

Let's now look at Disciple B. If the scribe was overeager, Disciple B is "undereager." Before evaluating this exchange, Jesus' response to this person seems to be a bit off-putting. That's when understanding the context will help us. It's possible that this man's father was not even dead yet. His commitment was conditional and delayed. Even if his father had just died, there was a funeral to tend to and then many months of mourning—in other words, he might have been saying, "Let me wait until my father is dead."[23]

What does Jesus' response to Disciple B tell us about allegiance to Jesus above all else?

Disciple B didn't understand that following Jesus isn't something you put off, no matter what pressing matters are at hand. We all have our reasons, though. When I'm not so busy, when God brings me a husband, when I'm an empty-nester, when I'm more financially secure . . . then I will follow Him. But the right time to follow is always now (Heb. 3:15). And allegiance to Jesus should always outweigh allegiance to even our dearest relationship. (The key here is recognizing that our most important earthly relationships will only be rightly enjoyed and valued when Jesus is first in our hearts.)

PERSONAL REFLECTION How do your earthly allegiances sometimes get in the way of following Jesus?

Let's continue reading Matthew 8:23-27.

Fill in the blank: The disciples _____ Jesus into the boat.

In light of the previous passage about the "would-be disciples," what is significant about the disciples' actions in this text?

The word *follow* is used in verses 19, 22, and 23, linking the passage about the "would-be disciples" and this passage together. We're to notice who followed Jesus and who didn't—the true followers are the ones in the boat with Him.

True/False: When we follow Jesus, it's always smooth sailing (v. 24).

Just seeing if you're awake.

After Jesus rebuked the winds and the waves, the disciples were amazed, wondering what kind of person could still the winds and cause the seas to obey.

Hold your finger in Matthew and read Psalm 89:8-9.

According to the psalmist, who is the only one capable of ruling the seas?

Back to the disciples in the boat with Jesus. What were the disciples beginning to understand about Jesus' nature?

Jesus' true followers were the ones getting a firsthand glimpse of His nature. They were beginning to understand that the One they were following, the One they were in the boat with, is the very Son of God.

It's infinitely better to be in a storm with Jesus than in calm circumstances without Him. Jesus' true disciples knew this. They didn't understand it all at once, though. They caught more and more glimpses of Jesus' nature as they ate with Him, listened to His teaching, prayed with Him, witnessed His miracles, followed Him through grain fields on the Sabbath, and took note of the alone time He spent with His Father. The disciples were learning the spiritual disciplines of Jesus without knowing that's what they were doing. They had simply taken His yoke upon themselves.

Turn to Matthew 11:28-30 for our final Scripture together.

The yoke Jesus referred to is a wooden frame that joined two animals together at the neck so they could efficiently pull a plow. Instead of that yoke being a contentious strain on the disciples, Jesus described it as being easy—also meaning well-suited and pleasant.

We follow Jesus not because He gives us everything we want but because He's worth everything we have. We follow Him because He has bid us "come." He is our true rest. Our truest home. And by learning from Him, by spending time in His presence and in the fellowship of believers, we become more like Him.

Though we are at the end of our study together, we are at the very beginning of a life rooted in the practices Jesus Himself lived and taught. As you've already experienced, the spiritual disciplines require effort on our part. But when we raise the sails of prayer, worship, Bible study, serving, thanksgiving . . . the wind of His Spirit carries us forward. And the regular habits that began as dutiful disciplines eventually turn into practices we can't live without. For we realize that it is in these practices that we encounter God.

Fellowship, Confession, Submission, and Service

FELLOWSHIP

We were not built for isolation. That is confirmed throughout Scripture, starting in the garden. So be intentional about being with other believers.

WHY?

- We need the encouragement and support.

- We need appropriate physical touch—handshakes, hugs, a hand on our shoulder.

- We need the accountability.

- We need to suffer together and rejoice together—these are not meant to be solo experiences.

HOW?

- Don't just slip in and out of a church service, but get involved in your local church. Attending a service once a week or a couple times a month can't be a substitute for meaningful relationships.

- Get involved in a small group Bible study or prayer group. It's great to go to church, but it's amazing the relationships you'll experience and the bonds you'll form by doing church with people, not just attending church. So find a smaller group.

- Get involved in ministry together. Serving for a purpose creates great fellowship. Some of my dearest friendships have been forged on mission trips or on serving teams, like when I used to lead worship on Sunday mornings.

- Create other opportunities, such as eating together. Great fellowship happens around the table. (See pp. 210–215 for delicious recipes.)

CONFESSION

Opening up and telling someone else about our sin, failures, or weaknesses is not something we long to do, but it is a freeing, strengthening, and healing practice. And it keeps us from living isolated. How do we do this well?

- Be willing to be authentic and transparent with someone who is safe and who loves and follows Jesus.

- For intimate sharing, choose a trustworthy, godly friend who will have your best interest at heart.

- If someone is sharing something with you, agree to confidentiality, unless permission is given to divulge that information. If you're confessing something to someone else, ask them to keep what you share between the two of you.

- Remember that you can be open and transparent without sharing all the details. This is especially important in a group setting.

- Ask your trusted friend to pray with you and for you so the enemy has no place to condemn or cast further guilt on you.

SUBMISSION

Practicing submission pushes hard against our natural sensibilities and the culture we live in. Our default is to answer only to ourselves, to be the "captain of our soul." Not to mention, we are regularly encouraged to put ourselves first. So how do we work this discipline into our lives?

- Submit to Christ first. We will never be able to make submission a habit in our lives without first coming under the reign of Jesus. Submitting to Him frees and empowers us to submit to others. It helps us see them through His eyes and love them with His love.

- Remember that submitting to others never includes submitting to abuse, degrading treatment, or dangerous situations. Not ever. Rather, the biblical examples and instruction about submission reflect an eagerness to consider the wants of others above our own, taking direction from another when it's right to do so, and laying down our rights for the greater good in certain situations.

- Pray for a heart of humility. Ask the Spirit to work mutual accountability and submission into your life. For instance, in my own life I don't submit to just anyone who happens to come along. I have trusted relationships with parents, a few close friends, my siblings, my pastor, and a few others. In certain situations, I have deferred to them even when I wanted to do something different, based on the good and biblical principle of submission.

- Practice putting others before yourself. Watch for opportunities to humble yourself and lift others up.

Keep in mind, as we practice submission more and more, it becomes a part of our character and will come more naturally to us.

SERVICE

All believers are called to serve. It's not optional.

WHY NOT?

- We are to follow the example of Jesus. Serving others was a lifestyle for Him.

- The Spirit has gifted you to serve. All believers have spiritual gifts to be used to help the church carry out its mission.

- The body of Christ can't be at its best if you're not serving. You are needed!

There's joy in experiencing the blessing of helping and encouraging others, just as there's joy when we're being served.

WHAT TO DO?

- When it comes to serving in the church, find a place to serve and get involved. Consider how you're gifted, what you're passionate about, what experiences you've had, and how God has created you. These will help direct you to a place to serve. We won't always be in the dead-center of our gifting, but we should be close if it's possible. For instance, I prefer teaching the Bible rather than sitting in board meetings. And I'm better at teaching. Don't feel like serving has to be drudgery. Lean into the gifts and resources God has given you.

- Practice a heart to serve. We're to be servants inside the church and away from the church. Your loving service to those around you will show them the love of Christ.

- See service as a lifestyle, not an activity or a project.

WATCH SESSION SEVEN VIDEO

DISCUSSION QUESTIONS

What's something that really stood out to you in the video teaching?

Why is community so vital to our Christian faith?

What has the community of faith meant to your spiritual life through the years?

How does understanding who we are in Christ affect how we live out Christian virtues?

Based on the definition Kelly shared about biblical compassion, who is the most compassionate person you know? Why did you choose that person, and how is he/she a picture of Jesus to you?

Why do most of us struggle so much with humility?

Why is patience, forbearance, and forgiveness so important in living out our faith in community?

Paul said that peace should rule our hearts. With so much turmoil in our world and lives, how is that possible? And why is it so necessary?

How is the teaching and admonishing that takes place in the body of Christ currently helping you in your faith walk? How are you contributing to this in others' spiritual lives?

Leader Guide

INTRODUCTION

Encountering God: Cultivating Habits of Faith Through the Spiritual Disciplines is a video- and discussion-based Bible study. The weekly personal study along with the teaching videos will promote honest conversation as you study Scripture together. Since conversation is essential to the experience, you'll find a few starter questions in both the Viewer Guides and the following Leader Guide to help get the discussion rolling. It's our hope that the added recipes will encourage groups to eat together because so many great friendships and conversations naturally begin around a dinner table. That said, this study may be used in a variety of large or small group settings, including churches, homes, offices, coffee shops, or other locations.

TIPS ON LEADING THIS BIBLE STUDY

PRAY: As you prepare to lead *Encountering God*, remember prayer is essential. Set aside time each week to pray for the women in your group. Listen to their needs and the struggles they're facing so you can bring them before the Lord. Though organizing and planning are important, protect your personal time of prayer before each gathering. Encourage women to include prayer as part of their own daily spiritual discipline as well.

GUIDE: Accept women where they are, but also set expectations to motivate commitment. Be consistent and trustworthy. Encourage women to follow through, engaging with the personal study, and attend the group sessions. Listen carefully, responsibly guide discussion, and keep confidences shared within the group. Be honest and vulnerable by sharing what God is teaching you throughout the study. Most women will follow your lead and be more willing to share and participate when they see your transparency. Reach out to women of different ages, backgrounds, and stages of life. This diversity is sure to enrich your conversation and experience.

CONNECT: Stay engaged with the women in your group between group meetings. Call, text, email, use social media, or send a quick note in the mail to connect with them and share prayer needs throughout the week. Let them know when you are praying specifically for them. Root everything in Scripture and encourage women in their relationships with Jesus.

CELEBRATE: At the end of the study, celebrate what God has done by leading your group members to share what they've learned and how they've grown. Pray together about what further steps God may be asking you to take as a result of this study.

TIPS ON ORGANIZING THIS BIBLE STUDY

TALK TO YOUR PASTOR AND/OR CHURCH STAFF: If you're leading this study as part of a local church, ask for your leaders' input, prayers, and support.

SECURE YOUR LOCATION: Think about the number of women you can accommodate in your designated location. Reserve tables, chairs, or media equipment for the videos, music, and additional audio needs.

PROVIDE CHILDCARE: If you are targeting moms of young children and/or single moms, childcare is essential.

PROVIDE RESOURCES: Order leader kits or download teaching videos and the needed number of Bible study books. You might purchase a few extra books for last minute sign-ups.

PLAN AND PREPARE: Become familiar with the Bible study resource and leader helps available. Preview the video sessions and prepare an outline based on the leader helps available to aid you as you lead the group meetings.

Visit *lifeway.com/encounteringgod* to find free extra leader helps and promotional resources for your study.

EVALUATE: At the end of each group session, ask: What went well? What could be improved? Did you see women's lives transformed? Did your group grow closer to Christ and to one another?

NEXT STEPS: Even after the study concludes, follow up and challenge women to stay involved through another Bible study, church opportunity, or anything that will continue their spiritual growth and foster friendships. Consider how you can provide future opportunities for your group to encourage one another in the spiritual disciplines and hold each other accountable.

SESSION ONE

1. Welcome group members to the study and distribute Bible study books.

2. Watch the Session One teaching video.

3. Following the video, lead participants through the Group Discussion section of the Session One Viewer Guide (p. 9).

4. Close the session with prayer.

SESSION TWO

1. Welcome group members to Session Two of *Encountering God*. Use the following questions to review the previous week's personal study:

Which day of personal study meant the most to you? Why?

How has God used His Word to guide you or instruct you in recent days?

What did James mean when he said we are to be not only hearers of the Word, but doers? What's your biggest hindrance in doing the Word of God?

What is something specific you know from Scripture you're not putting into action? What steps can you take to change that?

What does it mean that the Word became flesh? How does this truth reframe your understanding of Bible study?

What excites you the most about the discipline of Bible study? What are your fears and concerns?

What is something you found helpful from the How-To page?

What was your biggest takeaway from this week of study?

2. Watch the Session Two teaching video, encouraging group members to take notes as Kelly teaches.

3. Following the video, lead participants through the Group Discussion section of the Session Two Viewer Guide (p. 41).

4. Close: Entertain and discuss any lingering questions your group has about Bible study. Lead a time of prayer, thanking God for His Word and how He uses it to reveal Himself and make us more like Him.

SESSION THREE

1. Welcome group members to Session Three of *Encountering God*. Use the following questions to review the previous week's personal study:

Which day of personal study meant the most to you? Why?

Has prayer been more of a life-giving experience or frustrating endeavor for you? Explain. Why do you think prayer is a difficult discipline for so many?

How does understanding who God is help you pray bigger and bolder prayers?

How does praying for God to meet your basic needs put you in a posture of dependence on Him? Why is this beneficial?

Which of the four types of prayer (adoration, thanksgiving, confession, petition) do you most gravitate toward? Why? Which do you most struggle with? Why?

What excites you the most about the discipline of prayer? What are your fears and concerns?

What is something you found helpful from the How-To page?

What was your biggest takeaway from this week of study?

2. Watch the Session Three teaching video, encouraging group members to take notes as Kelly teaches.

3. Following the video, lead participants through the Group Discussion section of the Session Three Viewer Guide (p. 77).

4. Close: Ask for volunteers to share any big, bold requests they're asking of God. Take time to pray for each request. Depending on the size of your group, you may want to break into smaller groups for this closing.

SESSION FOUR

1. Welcome group members to Session Four of *Encountering God*. Use the following questions to review the previous week's personal study.

Which day of personal study meant the most to you? Why?

Why do you think it's important to express ourselves in worship?

How is our ministry and service for the Lord a form of worship? How is this taking place in your life?

What did you learn about fasting this week? Why is this discipline often overlooked, and why is it important to practice it?

How do you relate to the healing, rescue, and guidance the people were thankful for in Psalm 107?

What are some of your favorite ways to celebrate the Lord with others?

What is something you found helpful from the How-To page?

What was your biggest takeaway from this week of study?

2. Watch the Session Four teaching video, encouraging group members to take notes as Kelly teaches.

3. Following the video, lead participants through the Group Discussion section of the Session Four Viewer Guide (p. 111).

4. Close: Spend time together in worship and celebration. If possible, invite someone to lead a time of singing praise to God. Read Scripture. Shout. Kneel in prayer. Clap hands. Give your group freedom to express their authentic worship to the Lord.

SESSION FIVE

1. Welcome group members to Session Five of *Encountering God*. Use the following questions to review the previous week's personal study.

Which day of personal study meant the most to you? Why?

How has meditating on Scripture been a source of strength, comfort, and growth for you?

How and when do you take time to sit at Jesus' feet?

Why is remembering God's past faithfulness and work in your life so important to your present and future spiritual life?

Solitude provides you with time where nothing separates you from God's presence. How is that both inviting and unsettling?

How can you redeem seemingly insignificant moments of your day for purposeful time with the Lord?

What is something you found helpful from the How-To page?

What was your biggest takeaway from this week of study?

2. Watch the Session Five teaching video, encouraging group members to take notes as Kelly teaches.

3. Following the video, lead participants through the Group Discussion section of the Session Five Viewer Guide (p. 141).

4. Close: Encourage group members to find a quiet spot in the room, building, or outdoors. Consider giving them a passage

of Scripture to meditate on or prompts that would encourage a time of solitude with the Lord. Set a soft time limit and then meet back to discuss the experience. Close with prayer.

SESSION SIX

1. Welcome group members to Session Six of *Encountering God*. Use the following questions to review the previous week's personal study.

   Which day of personal study meant the most to you? Why?

   What would you say are the blessings/benefits and the difficulties/sacrifices of living simply?

   What areas of your current lifestyle hinder your ability to live generously and simply? How would living simply free you up to focus on the more important things of life?

   How can you practice generosity as a discipline?

   Do you normally take a Sabbath? Why or why not? What's the hardest part about stopping to take a rest?

   Why is taking a Sabbath so important to our spiritual lives?

   What is something you found helpful from the How-To page?

   What was your biggest takeaway from this week of study?

2. Watch the Session Six teaching video, encouraging group members to take notes as Kelly teaches.

3. Following the video, lead participants through the Group Discussion section of the Session Six Viewer Guide (p. 171).

4. Close: Allow a few volunteers to share their experiences and lessons learned from living simply and generously. Encourage them to share how these experiences have grown them spiritually.

SESSION SEVEN

1. Welcome group members to Session Seven of *Encountering God*. Use the following questions to review the previous week's personal study.

   Which day of personal study meant the most to you? Why?

   How important is spending time together with God's family? Why?

   Why are we prone to value our own comfort and success over serving and sacrificing for others?

   How does knowing you are uniquely gifted by Christ encourage you to serve? How does appropriate confession to trusted people help us live with integrity and keep us from living with secrets and shame?

   Why is it sometimes difficult for us to live in humility and submission? Why is it so important that we as Christians live this way?

   What is something you found helpful from the How-To pages?

   What was your biggest takeaway from this week of study?

2. Watch the Session Seven teaching video, encouraging group members to take notes as Kelly teaches.

3. Following the video, lead participants through the Group Discussion section of the Session Seven Viewer Guide (p. 205).

4. Close: Wrap up the study by encouraging participants to share key truths they're taking away from the study. Be sure to discuss how they will apply what they've learned and how you can help encourage one another in the practice of the spiritual disciplines. Share your gratitude for their participation in the study and offer a prayer of blessing over your group as you close.

Recipes

MOM'S BEEF AND VEGETABLE SOUP

You know I couldn't write a Bible study without including one of my mom's recipes. This was actually passed down from my grandmother. I don't think this recipe has ever been made the same way twice—you know, moms and grandmothers go by "feel." But I pressed my mom to write it down, and this is what she came up with. This is hearty, healthy, and goes a long way, which is a soup's specialty.

1 lb beef chuck roast, trimmed and cut in little pieces. (If you can find a piece with the bone still on, it gives good flavor.)

¼ cup flour

1 tsp. paprika

½ tsp. pepper and salt

2 Tbsp. olive oil

1 Tbsp. butter

½ yellow onion, diced (or 1 whole shallot)

3 garlic cloves, minced

2 bay leaves (Remove at end.)

4 cups beef stock (I use "Better than Bouillon®")

1 tsp. Italian seasoning

I large potato, peeled and chopped (about 1 cup)

I large peeled and chopped carrot (about 1 cup)

½ cup corn (1 fresh ear, or frozen)

2 cups chopped cabbage, chunked

1 large can of whole tomatoes (28 oz.)

DIRECTIONS

Shake the flour, paprika, salt, and pepper over the beef chunks. Heat olive oil and then add butter. Carefully add beef, but do not crowd in the pot. Do half the beef at a time. Add onion and garlic. Cook until translucent. Don't let them burn. Add the 4 cups of beef broth. Simmer the meat in the broth until very tender. Add more liquid if needed. While meat is simmering, cut up the rest of the vegetables and add them to the beef mixture along with the can of whole tomatoes. After it has simmered for an hour, take the tomatoes out with a slotted spoon and cut up the tomatoes and return to broth. (Whole tomatoes are softer than diced, which is why I use the whole tomatoes and cut them.) The soup is ready when the meat and vegetables are tender. Remove bay leaves. If your broth has cooked down, you can always add more to make it more soupy.

Lastly, my tips are . . . don't leave out the cabbage. If I don't have cabbage on hand, I won't make the soup. You can use rice or pasta instead of potatoes. My mother would put in potatoes as well as little broken pieces of spaghetti. I have a baggie where I keep leftover veggies so I can throw them in (green beans, peas, corn, and so forth). Some recipes are more tomato-ey with tomato sauce or paste. I like this with the thinner consistency of tomato beef broth. It's a soup, not a stew. You can use any can of tomato, but I like the whole tomato best. This soup is fabulous in the winter.

LIME TART

One of my favorite things about desserts in the Amazon is their use of sweetened condensed milk. It makes the dessert world go round there. My dear Brazilian friend and chef, Regina Pinto, adapted this light and creamy dish into a pie. You can't beat it in the summertime. And since one of the most important things about serving a dish is making people think it was harder to make than it actually was, the lime tart won't let you down.

PIE CRUST INGREDIENTS

2 cups flour

1 ¾ sticks of butter

½ cup sugar

1 egg yolk

Pinch of salt

FILLING INGREDIENTS

1 cup lime juice

Zest of one lime

28 oz. sweetened condensed milk (2 cans)

PIE CRUST DIRECTIONS

Preheat the oven to 350º. In a food processor, add the flour, butter, salt, sugar, and egg yolk until combined and the dough starts to form into a ball. Don't over-mix. Roll out the dough into a circle and place in an 11 inch tart pan. Blind bake for about 15 minutes until lightly golden. Remove from oven and set aside until cool.

FILLING DIRECTIONS

In a blender, mix all ingredients until very well combined. Pour the filling into the baked pie crust and refrigerate for 3 hours. Decorate with lime zest or edible flowers and serve chilled.

PEACH BRIE FLATBREAD

You can never go wrong with a snazzy and seasonal appetizer. Again, Regina for the win on this dish. She's taken some of our favorite ingredients like bread, peaches, cheese, and honey and combined them into this fabulous starter.

1 flatbread

½ cup homemade pesto or store bought

Brie cheese sliced into thin slices

2 ripe peaches thinly sliced

Olive oil

Salt and pepper

3 slices of prosciutto, torn

2 Tbsp. balsamic vinegar

2 Tbsp. honey

Parsley or basil for sprinkling

DIRECTIONS

Preheat oven to 400º.

Put the flatbread in a baking pan and spread pesto evenly over the bread. Arrange Brie cheese, peaches, and prosciutto and drizzle with olive oil. Sprinkle salt and pepper. Bake until prosciutto is crispy 18–20 minutes. In a small dish, mix honey and balsamic vinegar. Remove flatbread from oven and sprinkle some parsley or basil and then drizzle with honey mixture. Serve hot.

BANANA CINNAMON TORTE

Another nod to my Amazon friends and their love for the banana. Regina has given us another rich dessert with this one. Serve with vanilla ice cream or a cup of cold milk.

1 ¾ cups flour

½ cup sugar (plus 2 Tbsp. set aside for filling)

2 ¼ sticks unsalted butter

1 egg yolk

12 medium ripe bananas (peeled and thinly sliced)

¾ Tbsp. cinnamon

DIRECTIONS

Preheat oven to 350º. Pulse the flour, ½ cup sugar, butter, and egg yolk in food processor until the dough comes together, a bit crumbly like shortbread. Press the dough out into a 9x13 baking dish, about ¼ inch thick. You should have some dough left over for the top.

In a large bowl, combine the thinly sliced bananas, 2 Tbsp. sugar, and cinnamon and gently fold together. Spread the banana mixture over dough in the baking dish. It should come to the dish's edge. Press out remaining dough into creative patterns or just crumble on top. Cut a tablespoon of butter into tiny pieces and spread out across the banana mixture. Bake in preheated oven at 350º for about 30–35 minutes or until the crust is a light golden brown. Serve warm or cold.

ZUCCHINI AND FETA CHEESE CASSEROLE

This is a great dish to serve for brunch or at any morning gathering!

4 medium zucchinis, shredded
Salt and pepper
1 Tbsp. olive oil
¼ cup scallions, sliced thin
2 garlic cloves, minced

6 large eggs
¼ cup heavy cream
4 oz. feta cheese, crumbled
1 tsp. fresh thyme, chopped

DIRECTIONS

Preheat oven to 375º.

Toss zucchini with salt and let drain in strainer for 8 minutes. Press out excess liquid and set aside.

Heat oil in skillet over medium heat. Sauté scallions and garlic until softened. Stir in zucchini and cook until zucchini is soft and no liquid left in the pan, about 4–5 minutes. Beat eggs, heavy cream, 1/2 tsp. pepper together with fork until combined. Stir in zucchini mixture, feta cheese, and thyme. Transfer to a greased casserole dish and bake for about 20 minutes or until beginning to brown and eggs are set. Serve warm.

A Word from Kelly

1. John Mark Comer, *The Ruthless Elimination of Hurry*, (Colorado Springs: Waterbrook Press, 2019), 110.

Session Two

1. William W. Klein, Craig L. Blomberg, and Robert L. Hubbard, Jr., *Introduction to Biblical Interpretation* (Nashville: Thomas Nelson, Inc., 1993), 4.

2. A. W. Tozer, *The Pursuit of God* (Chicago: Moody Publishers, 1948), 87.

3. John H. Sailhamer, *The Pentateuch as Narrative* (Grand Rapids, MI: Zondervan Publishing House, 1992), 424.

4. Ibid.

5. James Swanson, *Dictionary of Biblical Languages with Semantic Domains: Hebrew Old Testament* (Oak Harbor: Logos Research Systems, Inc., 1997).

6. Elisabeth Elliot, *These Strange Ashes* (Grand Rapids, MI: Revell, 1998), 11.

7. "Shema," *Encyclopedia Britannica*, July 20, 1998, https://www.britannica.com/topic/Shema.

8. Eugene H. Merrill, *Deuteronomy*, vol. 4, The New American Commentary (Nashville: Broadman & Holman Publishers, 1994).

9. Richard S. Hess, *The Old Testament: A Historical, Theological, and Critical Introduction* (Grand Rapids, MI: Baker Academic, 2016).

10. Ibid.

11. Ibid.

12. Comer, 122.

13. C. S. Lewis, *Reflections on the Psalms* (San Diego, New York, London: Harvest Book, 1958), 63.

14. Peter C. Craigie and Marvin E. Tate, *Word Biblical Commentary: Psalms 1–50* (Grand Rapids, MI: Zondervan, 2004).

15. Amy Carmichael, *Gold by Moonlight* (Fort Washington, PA: CLC Publications, 1935, reprinted 2013).

16. Rick Brannan, *Lexham Research Lexicon of the Greek New Testament* (Lexham Press, 2020).

17. Spiros Zodhiates, *The Complete Word Study Dictionary: New Testament* (Chattanooga, TN: AMG Publishers, 2000).

18. Strong's G1721, Blue Letter Bible, accessed June 12, 2021, https://www.blueletterbible.org/lexicon/g1721/csb/mgnt/0-1/.

19. Douglas J. Moo, *The Letter of James, The Pillar New Testament Commentary* (Grand Rapids, MI; Leicester, England: Eerdmans; Apollos, 2000), 87.

20. Ibid., 88.

21. Ibid., 94.

22. Reuben Welch, *No Substitute for Persevering* (Grand Rapids, MI: Zondervan, 1983), 29–30.

23. Strong's G3056, Blue Letter Bible, accessed July 16, 2021, https://www.blueletterbible.org/lexicon/g3056/kjv/tr/0-1/.

24. Strong's H1697, Blue Letter Bible, accessed July 16, 2021, https://www.blueletterbible.org/lexicon/h1697/kjv/wlc/0-1/.

25. D. A. Carson, *The Gospel according to John, The Pillar New Testament Commentary* (Leicester, England; Grand Rapids, MI: Inter-Varsity Press; W.B. Eerdmans, 1991), 115.

26. Ibid., 127.

27. Ibid., 116.

Session Three

1. Oswald Chambers, "Greater Works," *My Utmost for His Highest,* October 17, https://utmost.org/classic/greater-works-classic/.

2. John Starke, *The Possibility of Prayer* (Downers Grove, IL: InterVarsity Press, 2020).

3. Ibid.

4. Andrew Murray, *The True Vine* (Chicago: Moody Publishers, 2007).

5. Bruce K. Waltke, *Genesis: A Commentary* (Grand Rapids, MI: Zondervan, 2001).

6. Kenneth A. Adams, *Genesis 1–11:26*, The New American Commentary (Nashville: Broadman & Holman Publishers, 1996), 36.

7. Strong's H430, Blue Letter Bible, accessed June 16, 2021, https://www.blueletterbible.org/lexicon/h430/csb/wlc/0-1/.

8. Robert D. Bergen, *1, 2 Samuel*, vol. 7, The New American Commentary (Nashville: Broadman & Holman Publishers, 1996), 70.

9. Beth Moore, Tweet, "Prayer was never meant to be all about answers. Prayer is taking God up on the miracle of access." February 13, 2020, https://twitter.com/bethmoorelpm/status/1227956564717236224?lang=en.

10. John Stott, *The Message of the Sermon on the Mount: Christian Counter-Culture* (London: InterVarsity Press, 1978).

11. Jonathan T. Pennington, "The Kingdom of Heaven in the Gospel of Matthew," Southern Equip: The Southern Baptist Journal of Theology, Spring 2008, 47 https://equip.sbts.edu/publications/journals/journal-of-theology/sbjt-121-spring-2008/the-kingdom-of-heaven-in-the-gospel-of-matthew/.

12. Leon Morris, *The Gospel According to Matthew* (Grand Rapids, MI: William B. Eerdmans Publishing Company, 1992), 144.

13. Craig L. Blomberg, *Matthew,* vol. 22, The New American Commentary (Nashville: B&H Publishing, 1992), 130.

14. Jonathan T. Pennington, *The Sermon on the Mount and Human Flourishing* (Grand Rapids, MI: BakerAcademic, 2017), 223.

15. Blomberg, *Matthew,* 119.

16. Scot McKnight, *Sermon on the Mount,* ed. Tremper Longman III and Scot McKnight, The Story of God Bible Commentary (Grand Rapids, MI: Zondervan, 2013), 180.

17. Ibid.

18. N. T. Wright, *Matthew for Everyone Part 1* (Louisville: John Knox Press, 2004).

19. Pennington, "The Kingdom of Heaven in the Gospel of Matthew," 47.

20. Robert Robinson, "Come, Thou Found of Every Blessing," 1758, https://hymnary.org/text/come_thou_fount_of_every_blessing.

21. John Stott, *Sermon on the Mount: Seeking First the Kingdom of God: 13 Studies for Individuals or Groups,* LifeGuide Bible Study (InterVarsity Press, 1987), 148.

22. Ibid., 149.

23. Ibid., 73.

24. Leon Morris, *The Gospel According to Matthew, The Pillar New Testament Commentary* (Grand Rapids, MI; Leicester, England: W.B. Eerdmans; Inter-Varsity Press, 1992), 149.

25. James R. Edwards, *The Gospel according to Mark, The Pillar New Testament Commentary* (Grand Rapids, MI; Leicester, England: Eerdmans; Apollos, 2002), 190.

26. Craig L. Blomberg, *Jesus and the Gospels: An Introduction and Survey,* 2nd Edition (Nashville, TN: B&H Academic, 2009), 72.

27. Murray, *The True Vine.*

28. Reuben Welch, *We Really Do Need Each Other* (United States: Impact Books, 1982), 58.

29. Tremper Longman III, *Psalms: An Introduction and Commentary,* ed. David G. Firth, vol. 15–16, Tyndale Old Testament Commentaries (Nottingham, England: Inter-Varsity Press, 2014), 221.

30. Ibid.

31. Strong's H1254, Blue Letter Bible, accessed June 16, 2021, https://www.blueletterbible.org/lexicon/h1254/csb/wlc/0-1/.

32. Ibid.

33. Ben Patterson, *God's Prayer Book* (Carol Stream, IL: Tyndale, 2008).

Session Four

1. Richard Foster, *Celebration of Discipline* (San Francisco: HarperCollins, 1978), 158.

2. Strong's H7812, Blue Letter Bible, accessed August 3, 2021, https://www.blueletterbible.org/lexicon/h7812/kjv/wlc/0-1/.

3. Ibid.

4. Johannes P. Louw and Eugene Albert Nida, *Greek-English Lexicon of the New Testament: Based on Semantic Domains* (New York: United Bible Societies, 1996), 217.

5. J. I. Packer, *Appreciating Salvation: Where Holiness Begins* (Ventura, CA: Regal Books, 2009), 69.

6. Warren Baker and Eugene E. Carpenter, *The Complete Word Study Dictionary: Old Testament* (Chattanooga, TN: AMG Publishers, 2003), 794.

7. Ibid.

8. Darrell L. Bock, Luke: 1:1–9:50, vol. 1, *Baker Exegetical Commentary on the New Testament* (Grand Rapids, MI: Baker Academic, 1994), 252.

9. Strong's G3000, Blue Letter Bible, accessed June 19, 2021, https://www.blueletterbible.org/lexicon/g3000/csb/mgnt/0-1/.

10. William Hendriksen, *Exposition of Paul's Epistle to the Romans* (Grand Rapids, MI: Baker Book House).

11. Dallas Willard, *The Spirit of the Disciplines* (San Francisco: HarperSanFrancisco, 1991), 167.

12. Ibid., 166.

13. Tim Keller, Tweet, November 22, 2018, https://twitter.com/timkellernyc/status/1065566310699024384?lang=en.

14. Leslie C. Allen, *Psalms 101–150 (Revised)*, vol. 21, Word Biblical Commentary (Dallas: Word, Incorporated, 2002), 88.

15. Foster, 201.

16. Welch, *We Really Do Need Each Other*, 34.

17. Craig Blomberg, *From Pentecost to Patmos* (Nashville, B&H Publishing, 2006), 25.

18. Ibid.

19. Robert H. Stein, *Luke, vol. 24*, The New American Commentary (Nashville: Broadman & Holman Publishers, 1992), 408.

20. Ibid.

21. Ibid.

22. Foster, 190.

Session Five

1. Willard, 162.

2. J. Oswald Sanders, *Spiritual Leadership* (Chicago: Moody Publishers, 2017).

3. Comer, 245.

4. Donald Whitney, *Spiritual Disciplines for the Christian Life* (Colorado Springs: NavPress, 1991).

5. Willard, 177.

6. Foster, 29.

7. Whitney, 306.

8. K. D. Weaver, *Meditate Like Jesus* (Eugene, OR: Wipf & Stock, 2018).

9. Dietrich Bonhoeffer, *Life Together,* (London: SCM Press, 2015), 60.

10. Ben Witherington, III, *Women in the Ministry of Jesus: A Study of Jesus' Attitudes to Women and their Roles as Reflected in His Earthly Life,* (Cambridge: Cambridge University Press, 1984), 101.

11. Ibid.

12. Madame Guyon, *Experiencing the Depths of Jesus Christ* (United States: Christian Books, 1975), 8.

13. Foster, 13.

14. Charles Spurgeon, *Holy Spirit Power* (New Kensington, PA: Whitaker House).

15. Bonhoeffer, 58.

16. Jackie Green and Lauren Green-McAfee, "The Praying Example of Susanna Wesley," faithgateway, June 5, 2018, https://www.faithgateway.com/praying-example-susanna-wesley/#.YNIQMjZKjxg.

17. Gerhard Kittel, "Ἔρημος, Ἐρημία, Ἐρημόω, Ἐρήμωσις," ed. Gerhard Kittel, Geoffrey W. Bromiley, and Gerhard Friedrich, *Theological Dictionary of the New Testament* (Grand Rapids, MI: Eerdmans, 1964–), 657.

18. William L. Lane, *The Gospel of Mark, The New International Commentary on the New Testament* (Grand Rapids, MI: Wm. B. Eerdmans Publishing Co., 1974), 225.

19. Ibid.

20. James R. Edwards, *The Gospel According to Mark, The Pillar New Testament Commentary* (Grand Rapids, MI; Leicester, England: Eerdmans; Apollos, 2002), 190.

21. Ibid.

22. Tim Keller, *Prayer* (New York: Penguin Books, 2014), 22.

23. Whitney, 226.

24. Comer, 130.

25. Andi Andrew, *Fake or Follower* (Grand Rapids, MI: Baker Books, 2018).

26. D. A. Carson, *The Gospel According to John, The Pillar New Testament Commentary* (Leicester, England; Grand Rapids, MI: Inter-Varsity Press; W.B. Eerdmans, 1991), 309.

27. Whitney, *Spiritual Disciplines for the Christian Life Study Guide* (Colorado Springs: NavPress, 1994), 27.

Session Six

1. Walter Brueggemann, *The Threat of Life* (Minneapolis: Fortress Press, 1996), 96.

2. Willard, 170.

3. Ibid.

4. Foster, 83.

5. Willard, 175.

6. Pennington, *The Sermon on the Mount and Human Flourishing,* xviii, 241–242.

7. Ibid., 239.

8. Crossway Bibles, *The ESV Study Bible* (Wheaton, IL: Crossway Bibles, 2008), 1990.

9. Willard, 175.

10. Eugene H. Peterson, *Christ Plays in Ten Thousand Places* (Grand Rapids, MI: William zB. Eerdmans Publishing Company, 2005), 110.

11. Ibid., 109.

12. Warren Baker and Eugene E. Carpenter, *The Complete Word Study Dictionary: Old Testament* (Chattanooga, TN: AMG Publishers, 2003), 980.

13. Ibid.

14. Merrill, *Deuteronomy*, 151.

15. Peterson, 116–117.

16. Derek Kidner, *Psalms 73-150: A Commentary on Books III-V of the Psalms*, (Downers Grove, IL: InterVarsity Press, 1975), 366.

17. Comer, 172.

18. *Mark: A Life Application® Bible Study* (Wheaton, IL: Tyndale House Publishers), 12.

19. Craig Blomberg, *Matthew,* 197.

20. Peterson, 110.

21. Strong's G2431, Blue Letter Bible, accessed July 6, 2021, https://www.blueletterbible.org/lexicon/g2431/csb/mgnt/0-1/.

22. This quip is often attributed to Abraham Joshua Heschel but likely traces back to a common Jewish saying.

Session Seven

1. William H. Willimon and Stanley Hauerwas, *Lord, Teach Us: The Lord's Prayer and the Christian Life* (Nashville: Abingdon Press, 1996), 28.

2. Welch.

3. Willard, 182.

4. Bonhoeffer, 21.

5. Craig L. Blomberg, *Jesus and the Gospels: An Introduction and Survey,* 2nd Ed. (Nashville, TN: B&H Academic, 2009), 71.

6. Gerhard Kittel, Gerhard Friedrich, and Geoffrey William Bromiley, *Theological Dictionary of the New Testament* (Grand Rapids, MI: W.B. Eerdmans, 1985), 448.

7. Bonhoeffer, 110.

8. Ibid., 117.

9. Bonhoeffer, as quoted by Stephen J. Nichols in *Bonhoeffer on the Christian Life* (Wheaton, IL: Crossway, 2013). 55.

10. Strong's G3875, Blue Letter Bible, accessed August 4, 2021, https://www.blueletterbible.org/lexicon/g3875/kjv/tr/0-1/.

11. Bonhoeffer, 113.

12. Willard, 188.

13. Willard, 190.

14. Bonhoeffer, 108.

15. Strong's G69, Blue Letter Bible, accessed August 5, 2021, https://www.blueletterbible.org/lexicon/g69/csb/mgnt/0-1/.

16. David L. Allen, *Hebrews*, The New American Commentary (Nashville, TN: B & H Publishing Group, 2010), 624.

17. Whitney, 144.

18. Ibid., 143.

19. Blomberg, *Jesus and the Gospels*, 385.

20. Whitney, 143.

21. Comer, 82.

22. Willard, "The Apprentices," interview with Dieter Zander, dwillard.org, accessed August 5, 2021, https://dwillard.org/articles/apprentices-the.

23. Blomberg, *Matthew*, 147–148.

ADDITIONAL STUDIES FROM KELLY MINTER

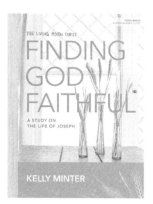

FINDING GOD FAITHFUL
A Study on the Life of Joseph
8 sessions

Trace the path of Joseph's life in the Book of Genesis to observe how God's sovereignty reigns, even in our darkest moments.

lifeway.com/findinggodfaithful

ALL THINGS NEW
A Study on 2 Corinthians
8 sessions

Study the Letter of 2 Corinthians to discover how God can use you no matter your situation.

lifeway.com/allthingsnew

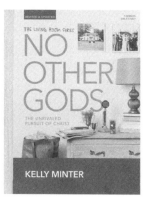

NO OTHER GODS
The Unrivaled Pursuit of Christ
8 sessions

Learn to identify the functional gods you may unknowingly be serving to experience the abundant life only Jesus can give.

lifeway.com/noothergods

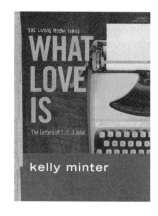

WHAT LOVE IS
The Letters of 1, 2, 3 John
7 sessions

Delve into the Letters of 1, 2, and 3 John, written to encourage followers of Jesus to remain faithful to the truth. Glimpse not only the heart of John but also the heart of Jesus.

lifeway.com/whatloveis

RUTH
Loss, Love & Legacy
6 sessions

Focus on the virtuous character and Book of Ruth to take comfort in her grief and struggles and watch as God rewards her faith and obedience.

lifeway.com/ruth

NEHEMIAH
A Heart That Can Break
7 sessions

Nehemiah's heart was so broken for those in need that he left the comfort of his Persian palace to help them. Are you ready to let God break your heart for a hurting, lost world and move you to be the hands and feet of Jesus?

lifeway.com/nehemiah

lifeway.com/kellyminter
800.458.2772

Lifeway women

Will you join Kelly
IN CARING FOR THE POOR, THE ORPHANED & THE FORGOTTEN?

Justice & mercy
INTERNATIONAL

Justice & Mercy International (JMI) is a Christ-centered, non-profit organization that cares for the vulnerable and forgotten in the Amazon and Moldova. Join Kelly, our long-time mission partner, in making a difference with JMI. **Scan the QR code** below or visit *justiceandmercy.org/cultivate* for more information.

Connect WITH JMI

Follow us on social media to keep up with the work of JMI.

f 🅾 @JusticeAndMercyInt   🐦 @JusticeMercyInt

LET'S BE FRIENDS!

BLOG

We're here to help you grow in your faith, develop as a leader, and find encouragement as you go.

lifewaywomen.com

SOCIAL

Find inspiration in the in-between moments of life.

@lifewaywomen

NEWSLETTER

Be the first to hear about new studies, events, giveaways, and more by signing up.

lifeway.com/womensnews

APP

Download the Lifeway Women app for Bible study plans, online study groups, a prayer wall, and more!

 Google Play App Store

Lifeway women

7-SESSION BIBLE STUDY FOR TEEN GIRLS

Encountering

GOD

CULTIVATING HABITS OF FAITH THROUGH THE SPIRITUAL DISCIPLINES

KELLY MINTER

ALSO AVAILABLE FOR TEEN GIRLS!

In this 7-session Bible study, teen girls learn how spiritual disciplines are essential to their faith and their everyday lives.

lifeway.com/encounteringgod

Lifeway.girls

Get the most from your study.

Leader kit, includes one *Encountering God* Bible study book, DVDs with teaching videos, and 3 additional teaching video downloads

Video teaching sessions, includes 7, 30–40-minute each from Kelly Minter

Audio teaching sessions, includes 7, 30–40-minute each from Kelly Minter

Teen girls Bible study book, includes 7 sessions

IN THIS STUDY, YOU'LL:

- Demystify spiritual disciplines and be empowered to practice them as you draw closer to God

- Understand how spiritual disciplines strengthen the Body of Christ, both in communities and individual lives

- Reframe your perspective on rest and renewal

To enrich your study experience, consider the accompanying *Encountering God* video or audio teaching sessions, approximately 30–40 minutes, from Kelly Minter.

STUDYING ON YOUR OWN?

Watch or listen to Kelly Minter's teaching sessions, available for purchase at lifeway.com/encounteringgod.

LEADING A GROUP?

Our leader kits are designed for leaders and make it easy to get your group started. (Leader kit includes one *Encountering God* Bible study book, DVDs with teaching videos, and teaching video downloads for 3 additional users.) Get yours at lifeway.com/encounteringgod.

Browse companion products, a free session sample, video clips, church promotional materials, and more at

lifeway.com/encounteringgod